Cuckoo Malware Analysis

Analyze malware using Cuckoo Sandbox

Digit Oktavianto

Iqbal Muhardianto

[PACKT] open source*
PUBLISHING
community experience distilled

BIRMINGHAM - MUMBAI

Cuckoo Malware Analysis

First published: October 2013

Production Reference: 1091013

Published by Packt Publishing Ltd.
Livery Place
35 Livery Street
Birmingham B3 2PB, UK.

ISBN 978-1-78216-923-9

www.packtpub.com

Cover Image by Prashant Timappa Shetty (sparkling.spectrum.123@gmail.com)

Credits

Authors
Digit Oktavianto
Iqbal Muhardianto

Reviewers
Charles Lim
Ashley

Acquisition Editors
Anthony Albuquerque
Amarabha Banerjee
Kartikey Pandey

Commissioning Editor
Shaon Basu

Technical Editor
Akashdeep Kundu

Project Coordinator
Akash Poojary

Proofreader
Kelly Hutchinson

Indexer
Priya Subramani

Graphics
Ronak Dhruv

Production Coordinator
Arvindkumar Gupta

Cover Work
Arvindkumar Gupta

About the Authors

Digit Oktavianto is an IT security professional and system administrator with experience in the Linux server, network security, Security Information and Event Management (SIEM), vulnerability assesment, penetration testing, intrusion analysis, incident response and incident handling, security hardening, PCI-DSS, and system administration.

He has good experience in Managed Security Services (MSS) projects, Security Operation Centre, operating and maintaining SIEM tools, configuring and setup of IDS/IPS, Firewall, Antivirus, Operating Systems, and Applications.

He works as an information security analyst in Noosc Global, a security consultant firm based in Indonesia. Currently, he holds CEH and GIAC Incident Handler certifications. He is very enthusiastic and has a good passion in malware analysis as his main interest for research. This book is the first book that he has written, and he plans to write more about malware analysis and incident response books.

Acknowledgement

I would like to thank Allah the God Almighty, my friend from IT Telkom, Indra Kusuma as a contributor and reviewer, and my boss and partner in Noosc Global for giving a facility for my research. I also want to thank my girlfriend, Eva, for her support and motivation in finishing this book.

I want to give you a list of names of persons to acknowledge as a gratitude for their effort in helping us in writing our book:

Chort Z. Row for the Video in Youtube (Using Cuckoobox and Volatility to analyze APT1 malware) at http://www.youtube.com/watch?v=mxGnjTlufAA, and thank you for providing Yara rules for Miniasp3 detection.

A.A. Gede Indra Kusuma from IT Telkom. Thank you for your effort in Malware Lab, and produce some resources for the book.

Jaime Blasco and Alberto Ortega from Alienvault. Thank you for providing Yara rules for APT1 detection.

David Bressler (bostonlink) for the great effort on Cuckooforcanari Project.

Alberto Ortega from Alienvault for his post on http://www.alienvault.com/open-threat-exchange/blog/hardening-cuckoo-sandbox-against-vm-aware-malware about Hardening Cuckoo Sandbox.

Xavier Mertens (@xme) for CuckooMX Project at http://blog.rootshell.be/2012/06/20/cuckoomx-automating-email-attachments-scanning-with-cuckoo/

All Cuckoo Sandbox Developers and founder: Claudio "*nex*" Guarnieri, Mark Schloesser, Alessandro "*jekil*" Tanasi, and Jurriaan Bremer. Thank you very much for the great documentation on http://docs.cuckoosandbox.org/en/latest/.

Mila Parkour from http://contagiodump.blogspot.com. Thank you for providing a lot of information about malware samples.

http://virusshare.com/ and http://virusshare.com/ for providing us APT1 malware sample.

Iqbal Muhardianto is a security enthusiast and he is working in the Ministry of Foreign Affairs of the Republic of Indonesia. He loves breaking things apart just to know how it works. In his computer learning career, he first started with learning MS-DOS and some C programming, after being a System admin, Network Admin, and now he is a IT Security Administrator with some skills in Linux, Windows, Network, SIEM, Malware Analysis, and Pentesting.

He currently lives Norway and works as an IT Staff in the Indonesia Embassy in Oslo.

I would like to thank Allah the God Almighty, my parents and family, my friend Digit Oktavianto for inviting me to write this book, and my colleagues for their support and inspiration.

About the Reviewers

Charles Lim is a lecturer and researcher of Swiss German University. He has extensive IT consulting experiences before joining Swiss German University in 2007. His current research interests are Malware, Web Security, Vulnerability Analysis, Digital Forensics, Intrusion Detection, and Cloud Security. He has helped the Indonesia Ministry of Communication and Informatics create a web security assessment and data center regulation.

He is currently leading the Indonesia Chapter of Honeynet Project and is also a member of the Indonesia Academy Computer Security Incident Response Team and Cloud Security Alliance — Indonesia Chapter.

He is a regular contributor to the Indonesia CISO (Chief Information Security Officer) Magazine and also an editor and technical editor of IAES Journal.

> I would like to thank Packt Publishing for giving me the opportunity to review the content of this book.

Ashley has a vision to make Mauritius a free and safe Intelligent Island in-line with the vision of the Government of Mauritius. He has completed his Bachelor in Science in Computing from Greenwich University, UK, and his Masters in Science from the University of Technology in Mauritius in Computer Security and Forensics, where he has topped. He has shouldered important positions in Mauritius and is currently a senior lecturer and program coordinator of Information Technology at the Amity University, Mauritius. He has designed and developed several innovative courses ranging from Diploma to Master levels. These courses have proven to be highly relevant according to industry needs and are very much welcomed by all stakeholders. He has also contributed towards several government projects in the field of IT security. In addition to shouldering high responsibilities at Amity, Ashley is a heavily sought consultant in IT security. Mr. Paupiah is of the opinion that he has acquired and mastered most of the tools required to achieve his vision.

www.PacktPub.com

Support files, eBooks, discount offers and more

You might want to visit www.PacktPub.com for support files and downloads related to your book.

Did you know that Packt offers eBook versions of every book published, with PDF and ePub files available? You can upgrade to the eBook version at www.PacktPub.com and as a print book customer, you are entitled to a discount on the eBook copy. Get in touch with us at service@packtpub.com for more details.

At www.PacktPub.com, you can also read a collection of free technical articles, sign up for a range of free newsletters and receive exclusive discounts and offers on Packt books and eBooks.

http://PacktLib.PacktPub.com

Do you need instant solutions to your IT questions? PacktLib is Packt's online digital book library. Here, you can access, read and search across Packt's entire library of books.

Why Subscribe?

- Fully searchable across every book published by Packt
- Copy and paste, print and bookmark content
- On demand and accessible via web browser

Free Access for Packt account holders

If you have an account with Packt at www.PacktPub.com, you can use this to access PacktLib today and view nine entirely free books. Simply use your login credentials for immediate access.

Table of Contents

Preface

Welcome to *Cuckoo Malware Analysis*. This book has especially been created to provide you with all the information you need to get set up with Cuckoo Sandbox. In this book, you will learn the basics of malware analysis using Cuckoo Sandbox, get started with submitting your first malware sample, and create a report from it. You will also find out some tips and tricks for using Cuckoo Sandbox.

What this book covers

Chapter 1, Getting Started with Automated Malware Analysis using Cuckoo Sandbox, gets you started with the basic installation of Cuckoo Sandbox and teaches you the basic theory in Sandboxing, how to prepare a safe environment lab for malware analysis, and troubleshoot some problems after installing Cuckoo Sandbox.

Chapter 2, Using Cuckoo Sandbox to Analyze a Sample Malware, teaches you how to use Cuckoo Sandbox and its features, how to analyze sample malicious PDF files or malicious URLs, and also covers some basics of memory forensic analysis with Cuckoo Sandbox and Volatility.

Chapter 3, Analyzing Output of Cuckoo Sandbox, will help you analyze the results from Cuckoo sandbox, demonstrate the ability to analyze memory dump in a forensic process, and simulate an analysis of a sample APT attack in collaboration with other tools such as Volatility, Yara, Wireshark, Radare, and Bokken. This chapter will also help users analyze the output from Cuckoo Sandbox more easily and clearly.

Chapter 4, Reporting with Cuckoo Sandbox, will teach you how to create a malware analysis report using Cuckoo Sandbox reporting tools and export the output data report to another format for advanced report analysis. It will start with human-readable format (TXT and HTML), MAEC format (MITRE standard format), and the ability to export a data report to the most useful format in the world (PDF).

Chapter 5, Tips and Tricks for Cuckoo Sandbox, provides you with some tips and tricks for enhancing Cuckoo's analyzing abilities during the malware analysis process. Some people from the community created interesting plugins or modules that help users perform new experiments using Cuckoo Sandbox such as automating e-mail attachments scanning with CuckooMX, and integrating Cuckoo Sandbox with Maltego project using cuckooforcanari. You will also learn how to harden your VM environment for malware analysis.

What you need for this book

An Ubuntu 12.04 LTS or newer, VirtualBox 4.2.16 or newer, some malware samples, and an Internet connection.

Who this book is for

This book is great for someone who wants to start learning malware analysis easily without requiring much technical skills. The readers will go through learning some basic knowledge in programming, networking, disassembling, forensics, and virtualization along with malware analysis.

Conventions

In this book, you will find a number of styles of text that distinguish between different kinds of information. Here are some examples of these styles, and an explanation of their meaning.

Code words in text, database table names, folder names, filenames, file extensions, pathnames, dummy URLs, user inputs, and Twitter handles are shown as follows: "Nevertheless, we will try to compile the `cuckoomon.dll` source code with the file we had changed before (`hook.reg.c`)."

Any command-line input or output is written as follows:

```
$ sudo apt-get install radare radare2 bokken pyew
```

New terms and **important words** are shown in bold. Words that you see on the screen, in menus or dialog boxes for example, appear in the text like this: "According to the **Installation** tutorial in the **README** file, it will work with a Postfix MTA."

> Warnings or important notes appear in a box like this.

> Tips and tricks appear like this.

Reader feedback

Feedback from our readers is always welcome. Let us know what you think about this book—what you liked or may have disliked. Reader feedback is important for us to develop titles that you really get the most out of.

To send us general feedback, simply send an e-mail to feedback@packtpub.com, and mention the book title through the subject of your message.

If there is a topic that you have expertise in and you are interested in either writing or contributing to a book, see our author guide on www.packtpub.com/authors.

Customer support

Now that you are the proud owner of a Packt book, we have a number of things to help you to get the most from your purchase.

Downloading the example code

You can download the example code files for all Packt books you have purchased from your account at http://www.packtpub.com. If you purchased this book elsewhere, you can visit http://www.packtpub.com/support and register to have the files e-mailed directly to you.

Errata

Although we have taken every care to ensure the accuracy of our content, mistakes do happen. If you find a mistake in one of our books—maybe a mistake in the text or the code—we would be grateful if you would report this to us. By doing so, you can save other readers from frustration and help us improve subsequent versions of this book. If you find any errata, please report them by visiting http://www.packtpub.com/support, selecting your book, clicking on the **errata submission form** link, and entering the details of your errata. Once your errata are verified, your submission will be accepted and the errata will be uploaded to our website, or added to any list of existing errata, under the Errata section of that title.

Piracy

Piracy of copyright material on the Internet is an ongoing problem across all media. At Packt, we take the protection of our copyright and licenses very seriously. If you come across any illegal copies of our works, in any form, on the Internet, please provide us with the location address or website name immediately so that we can pursue a remedy.

Please contact us at copyright@packtpub.com with a link to the suspected pirated material.

We appreciate your help in protecting our authors, and our ability to bring you valuable content.

Questions

You can contact us at questions@packtpub.com if you are having a problem with any aspect of the book, and we will do our best to address it.

1
Getting Started with Automated Malware Analysis using Cuckoo Sandbox

Malware analysis is a process of identifying malware behavior, what they are doing, what they want, and what their main goals are. Malware analysis involves a complex process in its activity. Forensics, reverse engineering, disassembly, debugging, these activities take a lot of time in the progress. The goal of malware analysis is to gain an understanding of how a malware works, so that we can protect our organization by preventing malware attacks.

Malware analysis methodologies

There are two common methodologies of the malware analysis process commonly used by malware analysts: **static analysis** (or code analysis) and **dynamic analysis** (or behavior analysis). These two techniques allow analysts to understand quickly, and in detail, the risks and intentions of a given sample malware.

For performing static analysis, you need a strong understanding in programming and x86 assembly language concept. During the static analysis process, you don't have to execute the malware. Generally, the source code of malware samples is not readily available. You have to do disassembling and decompiling first, and after successfully performing reverse engineering you can analyze the low-level assembly code. Most malware analysts perform a static analysis at an earlier stage in the malware analysis process because it is safer than dynamic analysis. The challenge in static analysis is the complexity in modern malware, where some of the malware implement anti-debugging systems to prevent malware analysts from analyzing the pieces of code.

Dynamic analysis (behavior analysis) is a process in malware analysis that performs an execution of the malware itself and observes the malware activity. It also observes the changes that occur when the malware is being executed. Infecting a system with malware from the wild can be very dangerous. Malware infection on your system can cause damage to your system such as file deletion, change in registry, file modification, stealing confidential data/information, and so on. When performing malware analysis, you need a safe environment and the network should not connect to production networks. With dynamic analysis, you can monitor the changes made to the filesystem, registry, processes, and its network communication. The advantage of performing dynamic analysis is that you can fully understand how a malware works.

To handle the number of malware samples, some automated malware analysis techniques have been developed. Automating some aspects of malware analysis is critical for organizations processing large numbers of malicious programs. Automation will allow analysts to focus more on the tasks that need more attention in human analysis.

When using **Cuckoo** as an automated malware analysis tool, it is expected to reduce the amount of time analyzing a malware in a conventional way. There are some steps in dynamic malware analysis that require a lot of time; one of the instances are while we're setting up a virtualized environment for a malware to run. The process may seem easy, but if we have several malware to analyze, it will be pretty time-consuming.

Basic theory in Sandboxing

As malware became more sophisticated, we needed more technology that would allow us to analyze malware easily without compromising our system. One such technology that can be used is **sandboxing**. Sandboxing has a wide and various explanation among IT people. For a reference, you can see the explanation from Wikipedia at `http://en.wikipedia.org/wiki/Sandbox_(computer_security)`. In specific terminology (computer security), sandboxing is a technique for isolating a program (in this case, malware) by providing confined execution environments, which can be used for running unreliable programs from the main environment. To give a clear explanation about sandboxing technology, let's imagine a sandbox or sandpit playground for children. Sandpit is a container filled with sand for children to play. The "pit" or "box" itself is simply a container for storing the sand so that it does not spread outward across lawns or other surrounding surfaces. The children can do anything in the sandpits as long as they are still in the sandbox. By providing a sandbox, we can execute malicious applications and see the malware activities.

We can also analyze the malware safely and securely without worrying about the changes that will occur during the process. There are several malware sandboxes you can use for building your own automated malware analysis lab. For example, Buster Sandbox Analyzer, Zero Wine, Malheur, Cuckoo Sandbox, and so on. Cuckoo is the right tool to perform an analysis for a sandboxed malware because Cuckoo has a complete feature, it is fully open source, and has good support from its community.

Malware analysis lab

What is a malware analysis lab, and why should we build a malware lab? Malware lab is a safe environment to analyze malware. Basically, it is an isolated environment which contains a lot of useful tools for malware analysts that helps them in analyzing the malicious software. We should build a malware lab to be more proactive to new and modern threats that can suddenly attack our organization. It is also a form of advanced detection before antivirus vendors found a new malware specimen. The scope of the malware analysis lab can be determined by examining the processes that will occur in the malware analysis process.

Static analysis involves disassembling and reverse engineering the code of the malware. This can be done in a static state where the code is analyzed without being executed. No complex configuration is required for the lab, because actually you won't execute the malware itself. This lab is provided just to safeguard if you accidentally execute the binary malware when you are performing the code analysis. For dynamic analysis, you need to set up a more complex lab, as you need to execute the malware. Malware behaves differently depending on the operating system environment where they are being executed.

You should pay more attention regarding the location of malware analysis hosts on your network. Trojan, worms, and other types of malware can be self-replicating, so it's highly likely that simply running an executable code on a production network can lead to another machine on the same network being infected.

Setting up a malware analysis lab is actually quite simple and requires a minimum amount of hardware. Isolating your malware analysis lab from other computers in the network is not enough. In addition, you also need to isolate your lab from the Internet if you are not sure. You should consider this option, because sometimes a malware needs to communicate with the malware **author server**, for example, Botnet command and control servers.

There are two options in building a malware analysis lab, that is, a physical environment and a virtualization environment. As mentioned earlier, both of them have advantages and disadvantages. Building your physical lab will require a lot of money and time in building the environment as well. In this situation, building a malware lab using the virtualization technique will save your money and time. Virtualization software allows you to save the state of a virtual machine as it runs so that you can revert back to it when necessary. This term is usually called **snapshot**. Using this snapshots feature, you can have a virtual machine environment that contains an operating system with a full set of weapons of dynamic and static analysis tools, and then perform a dynamic analysis with the malware, and finally you can save the session using the snapshot feature so that you can load the initial infected state at will. After finishing your malware analysis, you can choose to save or discard that snapshot and revert back to a clean image. Then, using the snapshot feature, you do not have to worry about malware that will infect your Guest OS, as you will be able to easily restore to the previous state.

From now on, you can be aware that the automated analyses of malware, which uses virtualization in operating systems, will help you to shorten the time in analyzing malware samples. Virtualization technologies have become a key component in automated malware analyses because of the cost effectiveness in hardware consumption and CPU resource utilization. By using a popular operating system and intentionally infecting it with a captured malware sample, it is generally useful to monitor the activities of the malware and determine the suspicious activities that occurs. The drawback of implementing automated malware analysis is that this method can be easily detected by malware writers as it frequently uses evasion techniques such as anti-debugging, packers, encryption, obfuscating code, and so on. But you can try to hide as many virtualization traces as possible. There is a lot of information on the Internet regarding virtualization detection techniques and countermeasures of malware analysis.

Cuckoo Sandbox

As described in its official website (http://www.cuckoosandbox.org/), Cuckoo is a malware sandboxing utility which has practical applications of the dynamical analysis approach. Instead of statically analyzing the binary file, it gets executed and monitored in real time. As a simple explanation, Cuckoo is an open source automated malware analysis system that allows you to perform analysis on sandboxed malware. Cuckoo Sandbox started as a Google Summer of Code project in 2010 within the Honeynet Project. After the initial work during the summer of 2010, the first beta release was published on February 5th, 2011, when Cuckoo was publicly announced and distributed for the first time.

Cuckoo was originally designed and developed by Claudio "nex" Guarnieri, who is still the main developer and coordinates all efforts from joined developers and contributors. In March 2012, Cuckoo Sandbox won the first round of the Magnificent7 program organized by Rapid7. Cuckoo was chosen by Rapid7 for the first round of Magnificent7 sponsorships due to the developers' innovative approach to traditional and mobile-based malware analysis. Cuckoo is used to automatically run and analyze files and collect comprehensive analysis results that outline what the malware does while running inside an isolated Windows operating system. Cuckoo is designed for use in analyzing the following kinds of files:

- Generic Windows executables
- DLL files
- PDF documents
- Microsoft Office documents
- URLs
- PHP scripts
- Almost everything else

Cuckoo can also produce the following types of results:

- Traces of win32 API calls performed by all processes spawned by the malware
- Files being created, deleted, and downloaded by the malware during its execution
- Memory dumps of the malware processes
- Network traffic trace in PCAP format
- Screenshots of the Windows desktop taken during the execution of the malware
- Full memory dumps of the machines

Cuckoo Sandbox consists of a central management software, which handles malware sample executions and analyses.

Each analysis is launched in a fresh and isolated virtual machine. Cuckoo's infrastructure is composed by a host machine (the management software) and a number of guest machines (virtual machines for analysis).

The host runs the core component of the sandbox that manages the whole analysis process, whereas the guests are the isolated environments where the malware actually get safely executed and analyzed. The following diagram shows Cuckoo's architecture:

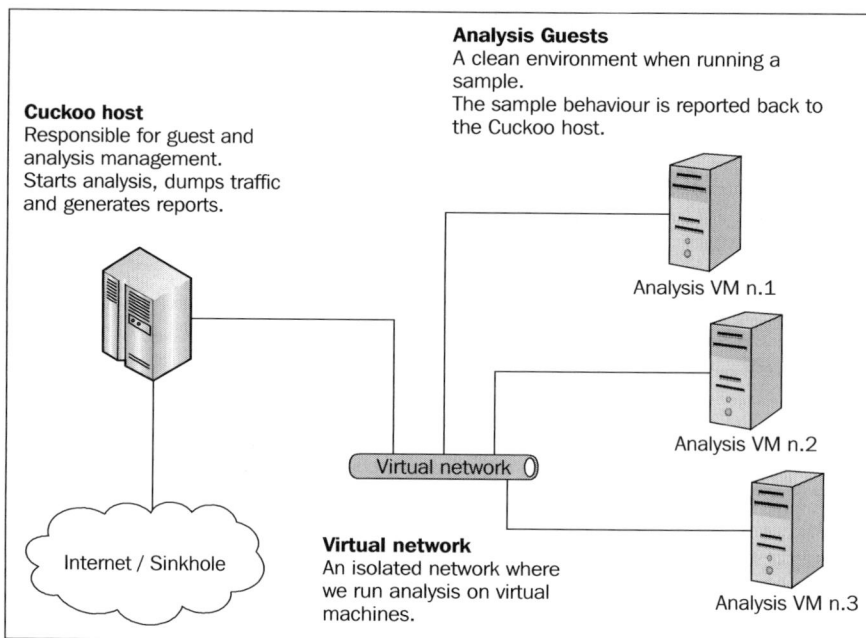

Installing Cuckoo Sandbox

Let us see what the important components are when installing Sandbox.

Hardware requirements

There are no specific requirements for hardware equipment. Requirements for minimum RAM is 2 GB (for virtualization) and free space in the hard disk drive of about 40 GB. In this book, I will use the following hardware specifications as the Host OS:

- Quad Core CPU
- 4 GB RAM
- 320 GB HDD

Preparing the host OS

Theoretically, Cuckoo Sandbox can run on every Linux operating system. In this book, all instructions in the Host OS will be conducted in Ubuntu 12.04.

Requirements

Before continuing to the installation and configuration process, you need to install some applications and libraries.

Install Python in Ubuntu

We need to type in the following command:

```
$ sudo apt-get install python
```

Cuckoo needs the SqlAlchemy application as the database toolkit for Python. So you need to install SqlAlchemy with the following command line:

```
$ sudo apt-get install python-sqlalchemy
```

You can also use pip command to install SqlAlchemy. **Pip** is a tool for installing and managing Python packages.

```
$ sudo pip install sqlalchemy
```

There are other optional dependencies that are mostly used by modules and utilities. The following libraries are not strictly required, but you should have the libraries to guarantee Cuckoo Sandbox runs smoothly in your environment:

- dpkt: This library is highly recommended and is used for extracting information from PCAP files
- jinja2: This library is highly recommended and is used for rendering the HTML reports and the web interface
- magic: This library is optional and is used for identifying files' formats (otherwise use the file command-line utility)
- ssdeep: This library is also optional and is used for calculating fuzzy hash or files
- pydeep: This library is optional and is used for calculating ssdeep fuzzy hash of files

- `pymongo`: This library is optional and is used for storing the results in a MongoDB database

- `yara` and `yara python`: This library is optional and is used for matching Yara signatures (use the svn version)

- `libvirt`: This library is optional and it uses the KVM machine manager

- `bottlepy`: This library is optional and it uses the `web.py` and `api.py` utilities

- `pefile`: This library is optional and is used for static analysis of PE32 binaries

All the packages can be installed by using a one-line `apt-get` command:

```
$ sudo apt-get install python-dpkt python-jinja2 python-magic
python-pymongo python-libvirt python-bottle python-pefile ssdeep
```

Or you can install all the packages using `pip` package management (except `python-magic` and `python-libvirt`):

```
$ sudo pip install dpkt jinja2 pymongo bottle pefile
```

You have to install `pydeep` for `ssdeep` fuzzy hashes of samples; but before installing `Pydeep`, we need to install some dependencies with the following command line:

- Build-essential
- Git
- Libpcre3
- Libpcre3-dev
- Libpcre++-dev

```
$ sudo apt-get install build-essential git libpcre3 libpcre3-dev
libpcre++-dev
```

Next, you have to clone `pydeep` from the the `git` source (put `pydeep` in the `/opt` folder):

```
$ cd /opt
$ git clone https://github.com/kbandla/pydeep.git pydeep
$ cd /opt/pydeep/
python setup.py build
sudo python setup.py install
```

You will also need to install `yara` to categorize malware samples (put yara in `/opt` folder):

```
$ sudo apt-get install automake -y
$ cd /opt
```

```
$ svn checkout http://yara-project.googlecode.com/svn/trunk/yara
$ cd /opt/yara
$ sudo ln -s /usr/bin/aclocal-1.11 /usr/bin/aclocal-1.12
$ ./configure
$ make
$ sudo make install
$ cd yara-python
$ python setup.py build
$ sudo python setup.py install
```

You need to install `tcpdump` in order to dump network traffic which occurs during analysis:

```
$ sudo apt-get install tcpdump
```

If you want to run the `tcpdump`, you need root privileges; but since you don't want Cuckoo to run as root, you'll have to set specific Linux capabilities to the binary, as shown in the following command line:

```
$ sudo setcap cap_net_raw,cap_net_admin=eip /usr/sbin/tcpdump
```

You can verify the results of the last command with:

```
$ getcap /usr/sbin/tcpdump /usr/sbin/tcpdump =
cap_net_admin,cap_net_raw+eip
```

If you don't have `setcap` installed, you should install this library:

```
$ sudo apt-get install libcap2-bin
```

Otherwise (not recommended) run the following command line:

```
$ sudo chmod +s /usr/sbin/tcpdump
```

The `chmod +s` command means SUID bit. you add both user ID and group ID permission to a file. In this case, it is tcpdump. If you set the SUID bit "`s`" on `tcpdump`, then other users can run it and they will become the root for as long as the `tcpdump` process is executing. That is why this step is not recommended.

After you finish setting up the Host OS, you need to install and configure Cuckoo Sandbox in your Host OS.

Setting up Cuckoo Sandbox in the Host OS

In this section, you will set up Cuckoo Sandbox and configure it:

1. First, download Cuckoo from its website at
    `http://www.cuckoosandbox.org/download.html`.

    There are two ways to set Cuckoo up in your Host OS. You can either download the `tarball` file or you can clone from source using `git`.

    °   If you want to clone from `git` source, you can do this step:

        ```
        $ git clone git://github.com/cuckoobox/cuckoo.git
        ```

    °   If you want to download the `tarball` file from the website, you can visit the website and then press the **Download Cuckoo!** button.

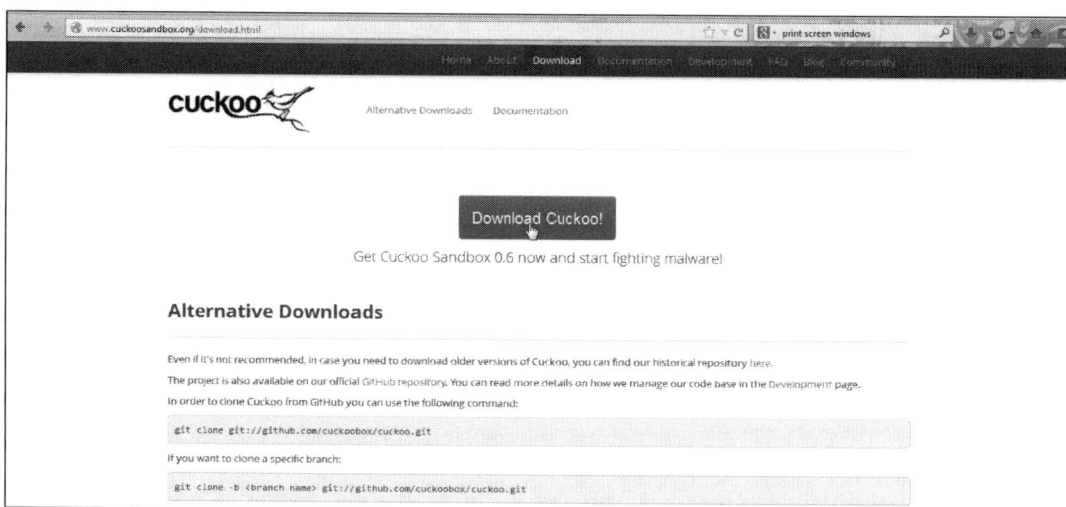

2. After you're finished downloading the file, you have to extract the files into a folder:

    ```
    $ tar -zxvf cuckoo-current.tar.gz
    ```

3. Before configuring Cuckoo in your Host OS, you need to set up the Guest OS, as the Guest OS will be mentioned in Cuckoo's configuration files (you will write down the Guest OS name in the configuration file). In this book, we will use VirtualBox Version 4.2.12 for 64 bit. You can download VirtualBox from the website `https://www.virtualbox.org/wiki/Downloads`.

In this book, we will use VirtualBox 4.2.12 for the Linux Host (If you can't find Version 4.2.12, you can use newer versions. But if you want to download Version 4.2.12, please go to `https://www.virtualbox.org/wiki/Download_Old_Builds_4_2`). There are several versions of VirtualBox for your Linux OS. We will download **Ubuntu 12.04 LTS ("Precise Pangolin") AMD64** version (this one is for the 64-bit version if you are using a 32-bit version, you can choose to download **i386**).

Before setting up your Guest OS in VirtualBox, you need to pay attention to Vbox driver. You need to set up vboxdrv first before creating your Guest OS. In order to set up the vboxdrv, you need to install kernel headers of your Linux. The kernel headers will be required in compiling vboxdrv. If you want to be sure about your kernel version, you can use this command:

```
$ uname -a
```

You will see an output like this:

```
Linux digit-labs 3.5.0.17-generic #28-ubuntu SMP Tue Oct 9 19:31:23 UTC
2012 x86_64x86_64 x86_64 x86_64 GNU/Linux
```

It means you are using kernel Version 3.5.0.17, and you need to install the kernel headers using this command:

```
$ apt-get install linux-headers-3.5.0.17-generic
```

After you're finished installing the Linux headers, you can set up vboxdrv with the following command lines:

```
$ sudo /etc/init.d/vboxdrv setup
* Stopping VirtualBox kernel modules            [OK]
* Recompiling VirtualBox kernel modules         [OK]
* Starting VirtualBox kernel modules            [OK]
```

If all the output is **OK**, it means you can now set up the Guest OS.

Preparing the Guest OS

The required specifications to set up the Guest OS are listed as follows:

- 1GB RAM memory
- 10 GB of hard disk space
- VDI format for the virtual disk
- Dynamically allocated storage
- Windows XP SP3

> When you are installing the Guest OS, you have to create the Guest OS name for the Cuckoo Sandbox VirtualBox configuration file.

In the first step, we will create the guest OS. You can write down your guest OS name, and operating system type. Since we are using Windows XP as guest OS, you can choose Windows XP in the OS type and version.

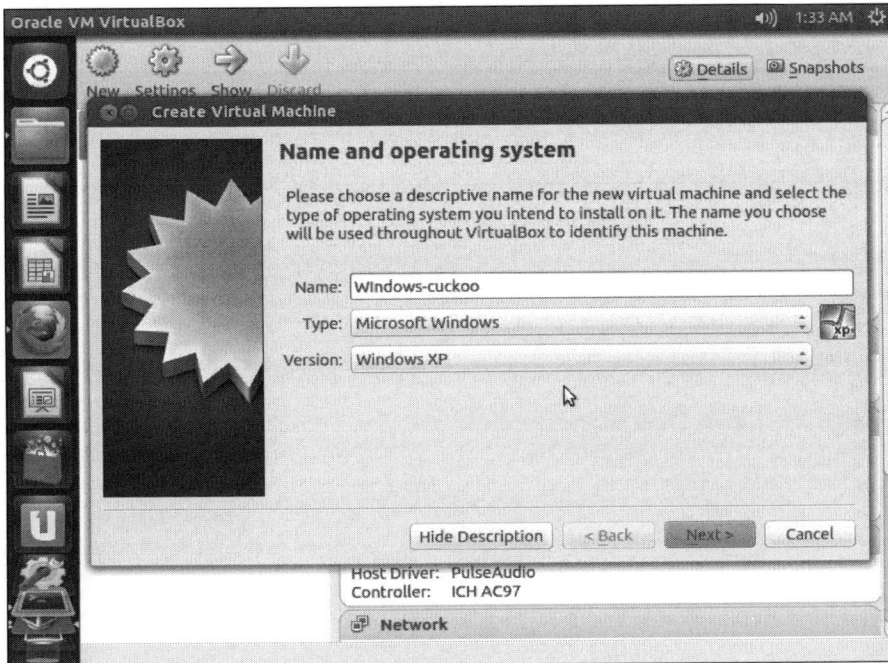

Before you start your Guest OS in VirtualBox, you need to configure the network, sharing folder, and the installing of VirtualBox Guest Addition to improve its capabilities in the malware analysis process.

Configuring the network

Basically, VirtualBox has several types of network configuration that can be used by the Guest OS. Each type has a different capability based on your need, we can learn more about it in the VirtualBox website:

```
http://www.virtualbox.org/manual/ch06.html
```

> Cuckoo is written in Python language, so you will need to install Python and other libraries as dependencies. Here is a website for you to download malware samples from, which will be used in this book:
>
> `http://www.cuckoosandboxbook.com/`
>
> You can download malware samples from the website. They will also provide you with some useful tools that can be downloaded from the same website. If you want to get additional information about this book, you can visit the aforementioned website, and put your comments there.

Based on the explanation in the website, we should use the **Host-only networking** type, because it will isolate our Guest OS from the outside network. With this networking type, Host OS and Guest OS can interact with each other, but the Guest OS can "see" the outside network or internet.

1. In the VirtualBox main window, click on the **File** button and select **Preferences...**:

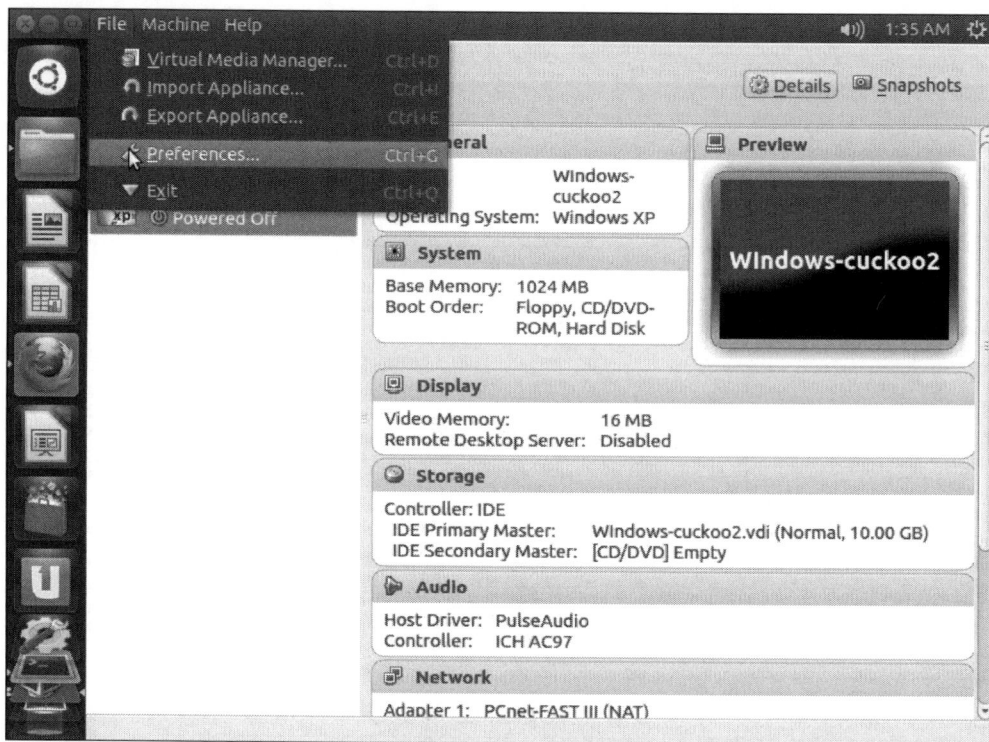

2. Choose **Network** in the sidebar to configure your host-only networking, and then click on the green icon that says **Add host-only network (Ins)** if you hover over it:

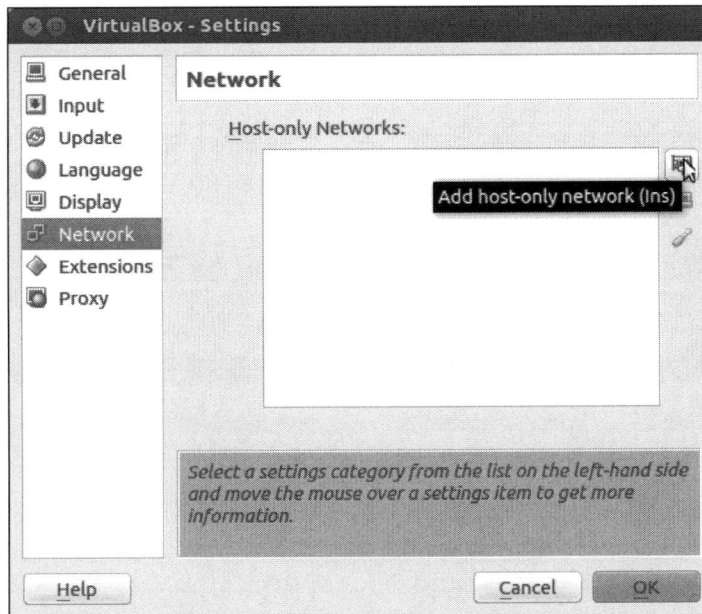

3. Click on the last icon on the side pane that says **Edit Host-only Network** to view your network configuration. If the DHCP server is not enabled, you need to manually configure your Guest OS IP Address but I suggest you leave it as it is:

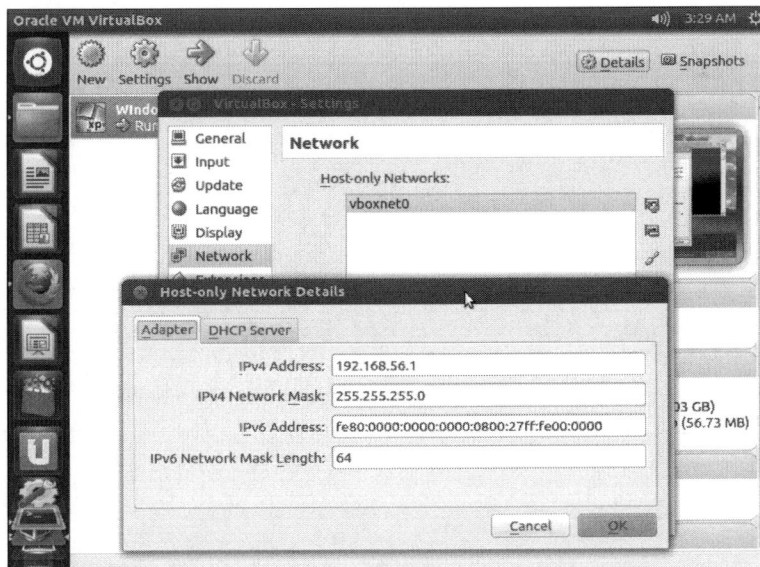

4. Next, you need to set up your Guest OS. Choose your Guest OS first in the sidebar, then click on the **Settings** option in the VirtualBox main window, and choose **Network**:

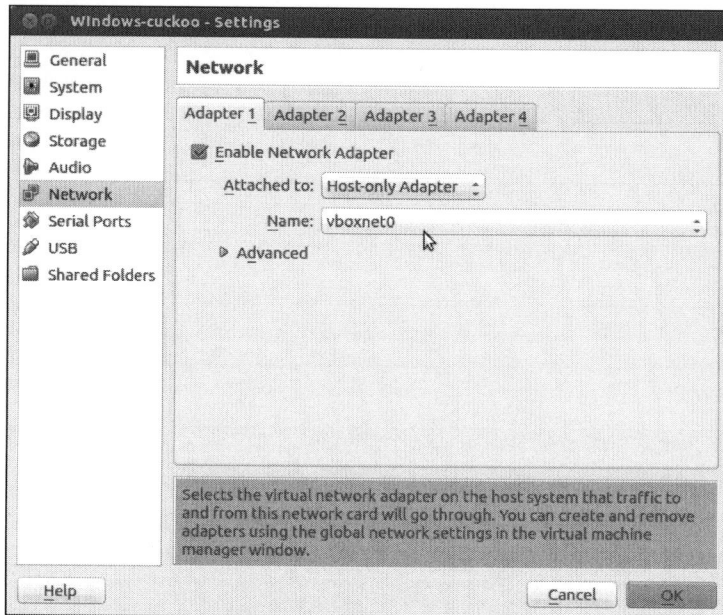

5. Go to the **Adapter 1** tab and tick the option **Enable Network Adapter**. In the **Attached to** drop-down menu, you have to choose **Host-only Adapter** and in the **Name** drop-down menu choose **vboxnet0** (network adapter name is based on what you have created).

6. After finishing your configuration for the Guest OS, you can start your Guest OS into the beginning installation process.

I assume that you have already finished your Guest OS installation process and logged in to your Guest OS. You will need to manually configure your Guest OS, as the DHCP server is not enabled in the host-only network configuration. Give your OS IP address with the same network segment as the Host OS. In this case, if you leave the host-only configuration as it is, the Host OS and Guest OS IP addresses will be set as 192.168.56.1 and 192.168.56.101, respectively.

Try to ping each other to make sure that the Host OS and Guest OS is already connected.

Setting up a shared folder between Host OS and Guest OS

1. In the Guest OS main window, click on the **Devices** option and select **Shared Folders...** as shown in the following screenshot:

2. Then click on the green icon at the top-right corner of your window that says **Add Shared Folder** (Ins):

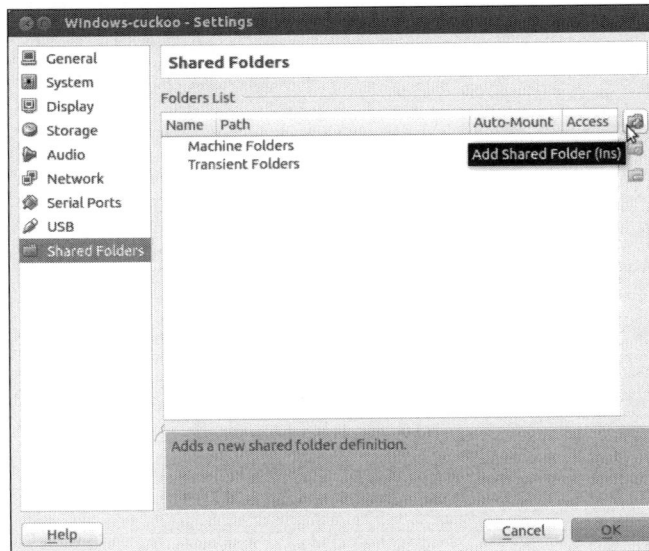

3. Choose the folder (in your Host OS) that you want to be shared with your Guest OS in the **Folder Path** (for example `/home/username/Downloads` or we can make our own folder somewhere else).

4. Give the shared folder a name (by default your computer will give a shared folder name, you can change the folder name as you wish), and tick the sharing options according to your choice:

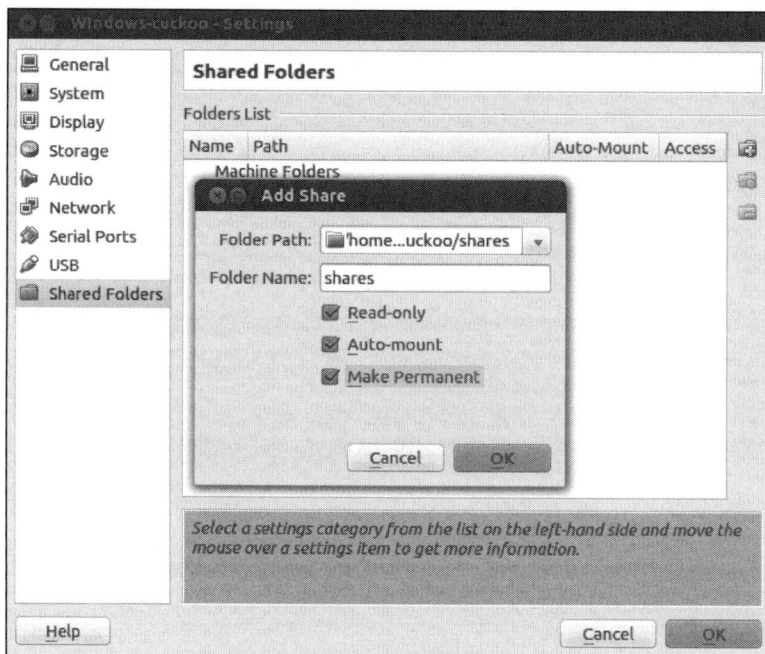

5. Now in your Windows Guest OS, click on the Start menu, right-click on **My Computer**, and choose **Map network drive...**.

6. Select the drive you want from the drop-down menu.

7. In the **Folder** text field, fill it in with `\\vboxsrv\shares` (`shares` is the shared folder name in the previous screenshot).

8. Go to **Computer** or Windows Explorer, and you will see the shared folder.

9. Now, to configure your Guest OS you have to:

    1. Install Python for Windows. You can download the software at `http://python.org/download/`.

    2. Install **PIL (Python Imaging Library)** Python module to created desktop screenshots. This software is available at `http://www.pythonware.com/products/pil/`.

    3. Turn off automatic Windows updates.

    4. Turn off Windows firewall.

    5. Install third-party applications (Microsoft Office 2003/2007, Acrobat Reader 9.5, Mozilla Firefox 3.6, and so on) at `http://www.oldapps.com/`. This step is optional.

10. Next, copy the Python agent to our Windows shared folder using this command line on the Host OS:

```
$ cp /home/digit/cuckoo/agent/agent.py /home/digit/cuckoo/shares/
```

11. From your Windows Guest OS, copy the `agent.py` file into `C:\Python27` folder.

12. Rename the `agent.py` file to `agent.pyw`.

    PYW files run the script without invoking the console window, especially if your program is GUI based. If you double-click the `agent.py` file, a command prompt window will appear on your desktop. If you rename the file to a `.pyw` file, there will be no pop-up window appearing on your desktop. It is similar to a background process in Linux.

13. To always run the `agent.pyw` file in startup process, you need to put it in the `Startup` folder in the following paths:

    For Windows XP go to `C:\Document and settings\username\Start Menu\Programs\Startup`.

    For Windows 7 go to `C:\Users\iKONspirasi\AppData\Roaming\Microsoft\WIndows\Start Menu\Programs\Startup`.

14. After executing `agent.pyw`, a new socket will be listening on the 0.0.0.0:8000 port. To check it, you should run this command in the command prompt:

```
C:\>netstat -aon
```

As you can see in the screenshot below:

15. You also need to configure Host OS IP forwarding and filtering rules using Iptables:

```
$ iptables -A FORWARD -o eth0 -i vboxnet0 -s 192.168.56.0/24 -m
conntrack --ctstate NEW -j ACCEPT
```

```
$ iptables -A FORWARD -m conntrack --ctstate ESTABLISHED,RELATED
-j ACCEPT
```

```
$ iptables -A POSTROUTING -t nat -j MASQUERADE
```

```
$ sysctl -w net.ipv4.ip_forward=1
```

16. The next step is the configuration of Cuckoo Sandbox.

Creating a user

You can either run Cuckoo from your own user or create a new one dedicated just to your Sandbox setup. We recommend you to create a specific user for your Cuckoo Sandbox environment. Make sure that the user that runs Cuckoo is the same user that you will use to create and run the virtual machines, otherwise Cuckoo will not be able to identify and launch them. Just run the following command line in terminal:

```
$ sudo adduser cuckoo
```

If you're using VirtualBox, make sure the new user belongs to the vboxusers group (or the group you used to run VirtualBox):

```
$ sudo usermod -G vboxusers cuckoo
```

If you're using KVM or any other libvirt-based module, make sure the new user belongs to the libvirtd group (or the group your Linux distributor uses to run libvirt):

```
$ sudo usermod -G libvirtd cuckoo
```

Now it's time for the best part, let's install and configure Cuckoo Sandbox.

Installing Cuckoo Sandbox

Extract or checkout your copy of Cuckoo to a path of your choice and you're ready to go. For example, we can put it in the /home/username/cuckoo path.

First things first, we need to configure Cuckoo's configuration files, which consist of the following main files:

- cuckoo.conf: This configuration file contains information about the general behavior and analysis options in Cuckoo Sandbox.
- <machinemanager>.conf: This file holds the information about your virtual machine configuration. (Depends on the name of virtualization that we used.)
- processing.conf: This file is used for enabling and configuring the processing of modules.
- reporting.conf: This file contains information about reporting methodologies.

The aforementioned .conf files are described in detail in the following sections.

cuckoo.conf

This file contains the basic and general configuration information of Cuckoo. For example, you can ask Cuckoo to check the newest version when it is being executed. If you use this feature, Cuckoo will download the newest version, and you can store the old version or delete it. It defines in the version_check on the `cuckoo.conf` file. You can describe your virtualization method in the `cuckoo.conf` file. For example, if you are using VirtualBox, you can write in `machine_manager= virtualbox`, or if you are using VMware, you can change this line to `vmware`.

You can also write down the Host OS IP address and port number that will be used by Cuckoo Sandbox. By default, the IP address is set as 192.168.56.1 (because we are using host-only networking method), and the default port is 2042. (Don't forget to define your networking interface.) We have defined the interface for Cuckoo, `vboxnet0` (look at the discussion about VirtualBox configuration in the *Configure the network* section).

<machinemanager>.conf

Machine managers are the modules that define how Cuckoo will interact with your virtualization tools. In `cuckoo.conf`, you will write down your virtualization software. If you use VirtualBox, the `<machinemanager>.conf` will refer to the `virtualbox.conf` configuration. If you use VMware, `<machinemanager>.conf` will refer to the `vmware.conf` file.

In this book we use VirtualBox, so you just need to pay attention to the `virtualbox.conf` file. You can edit this file based on your need. For example, if you want to run VirtualBox in GUI, you should edit the mode and set it as `gui`. If you feel comfortable using VirtualBox with command lines, then you should write down `mode = headless` in `virtualbox.conf`.

Remember in the Guest OS installation, I mentioned that you need to pay attention while naming the Guest OS because you will edit the Guest OS name in this configuration. Therefore, in the `[cuckoo1]` section, you can specify the Guest OS name. If you give your Guest OS name `cuckoo1`, you can edit `label` as `label = cuckoo1` (don't forget we created the Guest OS name `Windows-cuckoo`).

Since we are using Windows XP as the Guest OS, you have to define the `platform` section as `windows`:

```
platform = windows
```

Don't forget to write down the Guest OS IP address. We are using host-only networking, by default the first OS in guest system will be given the IP address 192.168.56.101.

processing.conf

This configuration file will allow you to enable, disable, and configure all the processing modules.

Basically, you do not need to make any changes to the default configuration in this file. But you can add your own VirusTotal API key in it. If you don't have a VirusTotal account yet and want to have one, just create an account in VirusTotal's website at `https://www.virustotal.com/en/`, and put the key in this line:

```
# Add your VirusTotal API key here. The default API key, kindly
# provided by the VirusTotal team, should enable you with a
# sufficient throughput and while being shared with all our users,
# it should not affect your use.

key =
a0283a2c3d55728300d064874239b5346fb991317e8449fe43c902879d758088
```

reporting.conf

The `conf/reporting.conf` file contains information on automated reports generation. This file contains information about the methodologies or kinds of reporting that you want to use after the completion of the analysis process. You can either disable or enable the reporting method.

After you finish configuring your Cuckoo Sandbox environment, you can test your first malware analysis process.

The virtual machine is now ready to test malware, but for the first time you need to create a snapshot file using this command:

```
$ vboxmanage snapshot "WIndows-cuckoo" take "WIndows-cuckooSnap01" --
pause
```

The following commands are used to restore the snapshot:

```
$ vboxmanagecontrolvm "WIndows-cuckoo " poweroff
```

```
$ vboxmanage snapshot "WIndows-cuckoo" restorecurrent
```

```
$ vboxheadless --startvm "WIndows-cuckoo"
```

The snapshot of the Guest OS is the most important part for the process of analyzing malware using Cuckoo Sandbox. Make sure everything is set and ready to analyze malware and carry out the following steps to perform the analysis:

1. To start your Cuckoo Sandbox, you need to run:

   ```
   $ ./cuckoo.py
   ```

   The output from your terminal will be something like the following screenshot:

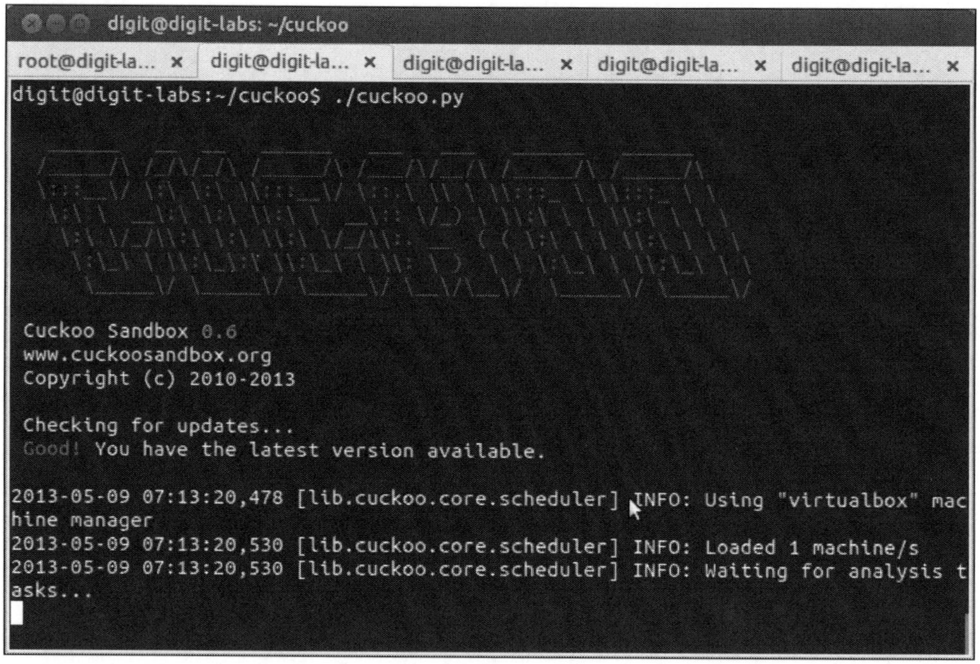

2. Cuckoo is now running and waiting for analysis. You can submit sample malware or malicious URLs. You have to change the directory to /cuckoo/ utils/ and then use the submit.py file to perform a malware analysis:

Then, the output from Cuckoo's main window will be something like the following screenshot:

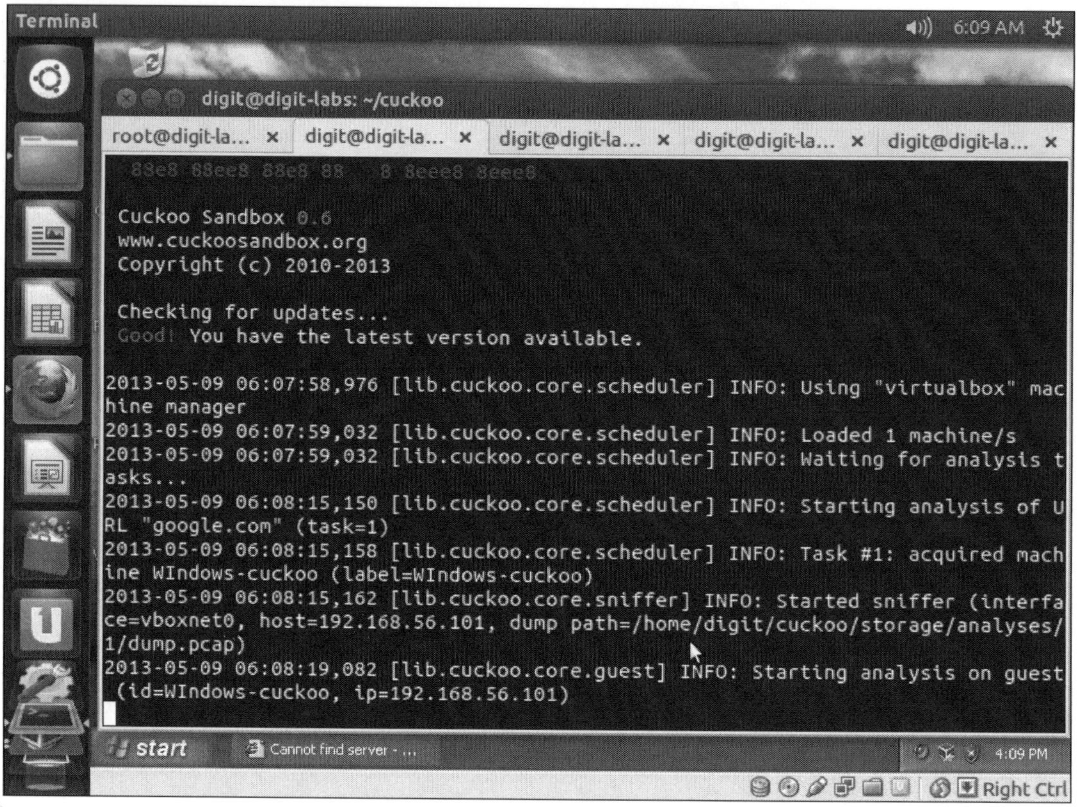

Summary

Now, you have successfully prepared the Host OS and Guest OS in the VirtualBox and then installed Cuckoo Sandbox. It is important to make sure that all the dependencies that are needed in the Host OS along with `pydeep` and `yara` are present. For the Guest OS, always turn off the defensive parameter and Windows firewall and use any software that the malware often use to interact with, for example, Adobe Reader 9.5, Internet Explorer 6, Microsoft Office 2003, and so on.

Always set your configuration in `<machinemanager>.conf` in exactly the same way as it is in the virtualization software you are using. For example, if you are using KVM, you have to set `kvm` in `machinemanager.conf`. Since we are using VirtualBox, you have to set `virtualbox` in the configuration. You have to be careful at the time of inserting the name of the Guest OS in VirtualBox to `cuckoo.conf` configuration file. For example, if you create a Guest OS named `cuckoo1`, you have to write down `cuckoo1` in the `cuckoo.conf` configuration file. The most important part of all is not to forget to make a backup of the whole system and configurations.

In the next chapter, we will continue learning about Cuckoo Sandbox's features, such as analyzing PDF files, URLs, and binary files, Memory Forensic using Cuckoo Sandbox (using the Memory dump feature), and additional Memory Forensic using Volatility.

2
Using Cuckoo Sandbox to Analyze a Sample Malware

The first chapter has explained about how to install Cuckoo Sandbox and configure the Host OS and Guest OS. In this chapter, we will cover the following topics:

- How to submit a malware sample
- How to analyze a sample of malware
- Memory forensic analysis in Cuckoo Sandbox

Starting Cuckoo

First, we must go to the root directory of the previously extracted Cuckoo. This time, the root directory is `home/user/Documents/cuckoo`.

We do not need to start VirtualBox to run the Guest OS (in this case, the guest OS is Windows XP SP3) in order to receive the malware sample. You must turn it off after configuring and installing some Windows applications mentioned before (for example, Adobe Reader, Microsoft Office, and so on). Do not forget to snapshot your current VM (virtual machine) — as it will be used several times — so that Cuckoo will start a fresh VM every time it runs the analysis. There are other ways to make the VM take snapshots. To do this using VirtualBox window, open its main window and click on the **Take Snapshot** button under **Machine**. (Snapshots can be taken when your Guest OS is started.)

Now we will start Cuckoo Sandbox. As explained before, type the following command line in the terminal and run:

```
$ python cuckoo.py
```

> cuckoo.py accepts some command line options as shown by the help usage:
>
> **cuckoo.py [-h] [-q] [-d] [-v] [-a]**
>
> Here is the description of the preceding command line:
>
> - -h, --help: When we want Cuckoo to show this help message and exit
> - -q, --quiet: When we want Cuckoo to display only error messages
> - -d, --debug: When we want Cuckoo to display debug messages
> - -v, --version: When we want Cuckoo to show the program's version number and exit
> - -a, --artwork: When we want Cuckoo to show the artwork

Please wait while Cuckoo Sandbox checks for updates on a remote API located at api.cuckoosandbox.org. In this state, Cuckoo Sandbox is ready for us to submit the malware.

Let's get our hands a little dirty, shall we? But first of all, make sure our environment is ready for some malware analyses. It depends on what kind of malware we want to analyze and on what kind of environment we are going to test the malware for a malware analysis to run smoothly. For example, if we want to run a PDF malware file, we should install Adobe Reader below Version 10. Try to download Version 9.5 from the Adobe website, they still have it:

http://www.adobe.com/support/downloads/thankyou.
jsp?ftpID=5336&fileID=4956

We can leave Internet Explorer 6 or 8 in Windows XP or 7 to analyze some URL or web files or maybe we can use Firefox 3.6 or Chrome 5. Just make sure the software we want to use isn't out of date. We can find such software on www.oldapps.com, www.filehippo.com, and so on, or simply just Google it.

There are a few important things to remember after you've finished installing the VirtualBox system in your Windows XP:

- Do not forget to turn off Windows firewall
- Do not activate Windows updates
- Never install any antivirus, anti-spyware, or any such software if you want the malware to run smoothly in the Windows environment

Submitting malware samples to Cuckoo Sandbox

For submitting malware samples, Cuckoo Sandbox has a command utility in its `utils` folder. To submit a malware sample run the following command in the terminal:

```
$ ./utils/submit.py [optional arguments] [positional argument]
```

As described in the previous section, we know that the arguments can be filled by:

- `[optional arguments]`:
    - `-h, --help`: This argument shows this help message and exits
    - `--url`: This argument specifies whether the target is an URL or not
    - `--package PACKAGE`: This argument specifies an analysis package
    - `--custom CUSTOM`: This argument specifies any custom value
    - `--timeout TIMEOUT`: This argument specifies an analysis timeout
    - `--options OPTIONS`: This argument specifies options for the analysis package (for example, `name=value,name2=value2`)
    - `--priority PRIORITY`: This argument specifies a priority for the analysis represented by an integer
    - `--machine MACHINE`: This argument specifies the identifier of a machine you want to use
    - `--platform PLATFORM`: This argument specifies the operating system platform you want to use (Windows/Darwin/Linux)
    - `--memory`: This argument enables the system to take a memory dump of the analysis machine
    - `--enforce-timeout`: This argument enables the system to force the analysis to run for the full timeout period

- `[positional argument]`:
    - `target`: This argument is an URL or path of the file/folder that is to be analyzed

> In this chapter, I will submit Cuckoo a few malware samples from the Internet. The malware sample that has been used in this book will be provided along with the book's code bundle at Packt Publishing's website. (REMEMBER! Do not execute the malware at any case in your Host OS. The risks and responsibilities of usages of the malware rest upon you).

There are some usage examples of submission utility using `submit.py` in Cuckoo Sandbox (for more information go to `https://cuckoo.readthedocs.org/en/latest/usage/submit.html`):

- For submitting local binary:

  ```
  ./utils/submit.py /path/to/binary
  ```

- For submitting an URL:

  ```
  ./utils/submit.py --url http://www.example.com
  ```

- For submitting a local binary and specifying an higher priority:

  ```
  ./utils/submit.py --priority 5 /path/to/binary
  ```

- For submitting a local binary and specifying a custom analysis timeout of 2 minutes (in seconds):

  ```
  ./utils/submit.py --timeout 120 /path/to/binary
  ```

- For submitting a local binary and specifying a custom analysis package (`applet/bin/dll/doc/exe/html/ie/jar/pdf/xls/zip`):

  ```
  ./utils/submit.py --package <name of package>
  /path/to/binary
  ```

- For submitting a local binary and specifying a custom analysis package and some options (in this case, a command line argument for the malware):

  ```
  ./utils/submit.py --package exe --options arguments=--
  dosomething /path/to/binary.exe
  ```

- For submitting a local binary to be run on a virtual machine named `WIndows-cuckoo`:

  ```
  ./utils/submit.py --machine WIndows-cuckoo /path/to/binary
  ```

- For submitting a local binary to be run on a specific machine (Windows/Darwin/Linux). In this case, we are using Windows:

  ```
  ./utils/submit.py --platform windows /path/to/binary
  ```

- For submitting a local binary and taking a full memory dump of the analysis machine:

  ```
  ./utils/submit.py --memory /path/to/binary
  ```

- For submitting a local binary and forcing the analysis to be executed for the full timeout (disregarding the internal mechanism that Cuckoo uses to decide when to terminate the analysis):

  ```
  ./utils/submit.py --enforce-timeout /path/to/binary
  ```

There is another submission utility of Cuckoo Sandbox using the web service. You can start it using this command:

```
$ python utils/web.py
```

```
devil@TheDevilInside: ~/Documents/cuckoo
devil@TheDevilInside: ~/Documents/cuckoo        devil@TheDevilInside: ~/Documents/cuckoo
devil@TheDevilInside:~/Documents/cuckoo$ python utils/web.py
Bottle server starting up (using WSGIRefServer())...
Listening on http://0.0.0.0:8080/
Hit Ctrl-C to quit.
```

The script will start a web server on your localhost using port 8080. After the web server starts, open your web browser and go to `http://localhost:8080`. It will prompt you to a simple form to upload the malware, specify some options (in the same format as the `submit.py` utility), and submit it:

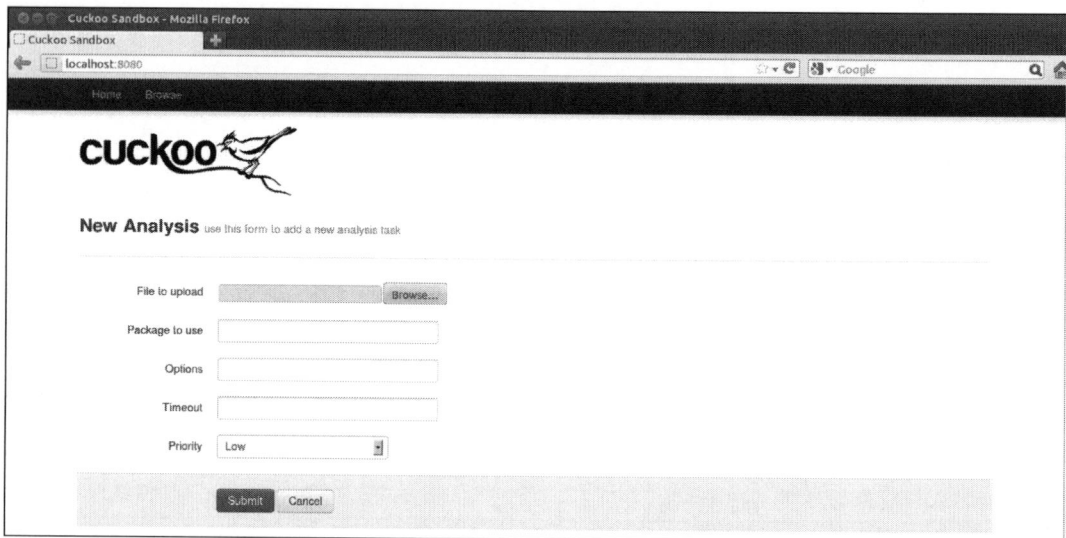

More submission utilities such as **REST API** and **Python Functions** will not be explained in this book. Those utilities are for developers and allow you to make the custom Sandbox that may use SQLite, MySQL, PostgreSQL, and several other SQL database systems.

> REST API is a simple and lightweight web API server implemented in `bottle.py`. Therefore, in order to make the service work, you will need to install it. You can see the documentation at `https://cuckoo.readthedocs.org/en/latest/usage/api.html`
>
> Python Functions may be useful if you want to write your own Python submission script. You can see the documentation at:
>
> `https://cuckoo.readthedocs.org/en/latest/usage/submit.html#python-functions`

Moreover, in this chapter we will submit three types of malware that are commonly found in our daily lives. There are many types of malware documents (for example, `.doc`, `.pdf`, `.xls`, and so on), malicious URLs, and binary files.

Submitting a malware Word document

This section deals with Word documents that contain malware samples. Please make sure that you have installed the Microsoft Office bundle program in your VM environment. Internet connection in your VM environment is also needed to make sure that the malware analysis can run smoothly in your VM environment.

We will submit a document dealing with *Iran's Oil and Nuclear Situation*. Perform the following steps:

1. Open a new tab in the terminal and type the following command:

   ```
   $ python utils/submit.py --platform windows –package doc
   shares/Iran\'s\ Oil\ and\ Nuclear\ Situation.doc
   ```

   In this case, the document is located inside the `shares` folder. You have to change the location based on where your document is.

```
devil@TheDevilInside:~/Documents/cuckoo$ python utils/submit.py --platform windows --package doc  shares/Iran\'s\ Oil\ and\ Nuclear\ Situation.doc
Success: File "/home/devil/Documents/cuckoo/shares/Iran's Oil and Nuclear Situation.doc" added as task with ID 7
```

Please make sure you get a **Success** message like the preceding screenshot with **task with ID 7** (it is the ID that depends on how many times you tried to submit a malware). Cuckoo will then start the latest snapshot of the virtual machine we've made. Windows will open the Word document.

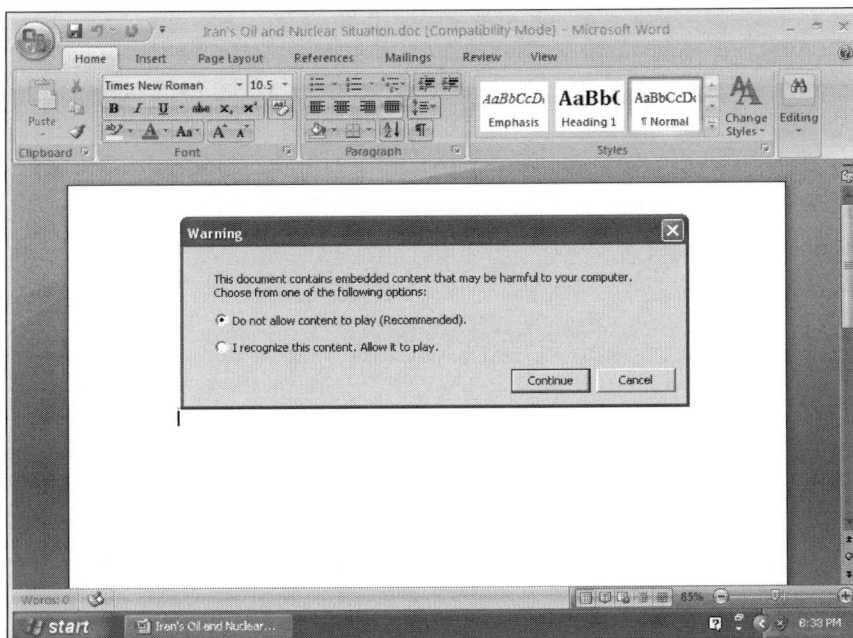

2. A warning pop-up window will appear as shown in the preceding screenshot. We assume that the users will not be aware of what that warning is, so we will choose **I recognize this content. Allow it to play.** option and click on the **Continue** button. Wait a moment until the malware document takes some action. The VM will close automatically after all the actions are finished by the malware document. Now, you will see the Cuckoo status—on the terminal tab where we started Cuckoo—as shown in the following screenshot:

We have now finished the submission process. Let's look at the subfolder of `cuckoo`, in the `storage/analyses/` path. There are some numbered folders in `storage/analyses`, which represent the analysis task inside the database. These folders are based on the task ID we have created before. So, do not be confused when you find folders other than 7. Just find the folder your were searching for based on the task ID.

When you see the reporting folder, you will know that Cuckoo Sandbox will make several files in a dedicated directory. Following is an example of an analysis directory structure:

```
|-- analysis.conf
|-- analysis.log
|-- binary
|-- dump.pcap
|-- memory.dmp
|-- files
|   |-- 1234567890
|       `-- dropped.exe
|-- logs
|   |-- 1232.raw
|   |-- 1540.raw
|   `-- 1118.raw
```

```
|-- reports
|   |-- report.html
|   |-- report.json
|   |-- report.maec11.xml
|   |-- report.metadata.xml
|   `-- report.pickle
`-- shots
    |-- 0001.jpg
    |-- 0002.jpg
    |-- 0003.jpg
    `-- 0004.jpg
```

Let us have a look at some of them in detail:

- `analysis.conf`: This is a configuration file automatically generated by Cuckoo to instruct its analyzer with some details about the current analysis. It is generally of no interest for the end user, as it is exclusively used internally by the sandbox.

- `analysis.log`: This is a log file generated by the analyzer and it contains a trace of the analysis execution inside the guest environment. It will report the creation of processes, files, and eventual error occurred during the execution.

- `binary`: This is the binary file we have submitted before.

- `dump.pcap`: This is the network dump file generated by `tcpdump` or any other corresponding network sniffer.

- `memory.dmp`: In case you enabled it, this file contains the full memory dump of the analysis machine.

- `files`: This directory contains all the files the malware operated on and that Cuckoo was able to dump.

- `logs`: This directory contains all the raw logs generated by Cuckoo's process monitoring.

- `reports`: This directory contains all the reports generated by Cuckoo.

- `shots`: This directory contains all the screenshots of the guest's desktop taken during the malware execution.

The contents are not always similar to what is mentioned. They depend on how Cuckoo Sandbox analyzes the malware, what is the kind of the submitted malware and its behavior. After analyzing `Iran's Oil and Nuclear Situation.doc` there will be four folders, namely, `files`, `logs`, `reports`, and `shots`, and three files, namely, `analysis.log`, `binary`, `dump.pcap`, inside the `storage/analyses/7` folder.

To know more about how the final result of the execution of malware inside the Guest OS is, it will be more user-friendly if we open the HTML result located inside the `reports` folder. There will be a file named `report.html`.

We need to double-click it and open it on the web browser. Another option to see the content of `report.html` is by using this command:

```
$ lynx report.html
```

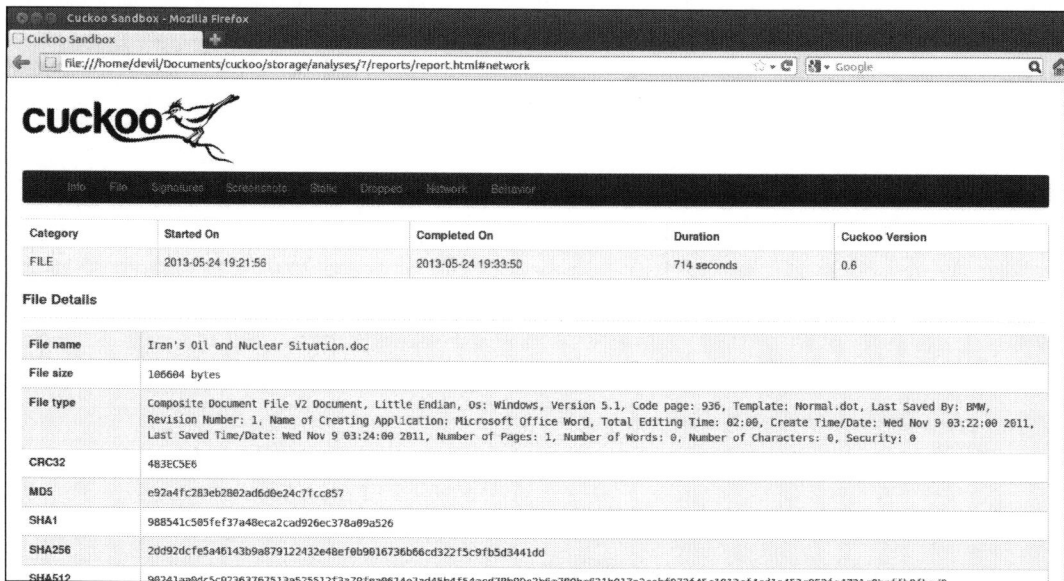

There are some tabs with information gathered by Cuckoo Sandbox analyzer in your browser:

In the **File** tab from your browser, you may see some interesting information. We can see this malware has been created by injecting a Word document containing nothing but a macro virus on Wednesday, November 9th, between 03:22 – 03:24 hours.

What's more interesting is that it is available in the **Network** tab under **Hosts Involved**.

Network Analysis
Hosts Involved
IP Address
192.168.2.101
192.168.2.255
192.168.2.100
208.115.230.76

Under the **Hosts Involved** option, there is a list of IP addresses, that is, **192.168.2.101**, **192.168.2.255**, and **192.168.2.100**, which are the Guest OS's IP, Network Broadcast's IP, and vmnet0's IP, respectively. Then, what about the public IP **208.115.230.76**? This is the IP used by the malware to contact to the server, which makes the analysis more interesting.

After knowing that malware try to make contact outside of the host, you must be wondering how the malware make contact with the server. Therefore, we can look at the contents of the dump.pcap file.

To open the dump.pcap file, you should install a packet analyzer. In this book, we will use **Wireshark packet analyzer**. Please make sure that you have installed Wireshark in your host OS, and then open the dump.pcap file using Wireshark.

We can see the network activities of the malware. We will further analyze this in *Chapter 3, Analyzing Output of Cuckoo Sandbox*.

Submitting a malware PDF document – aleppo_plan_cercs.pdf

In this section, we'll deal with PDF documents that contain malware samples and prepare to submit those. Please make sure you have installed a PDF reader application in your VM environment (I recommend you use Adobe Acrobat Reader). Internet connection in your VM environment is also needed to make sure that the malware analysis can run smoothly in your VM environment.

We will now submit a PDF file as a malware document. Let us see the steps involved:

1. Open a new **Terminal** tab (*Shift + Ctrl + T*) and type in the following command line:

   ```
   $ python utils/submit.py --platform windows --package pdf
   shares/aleppo_plan_cercs.pdf
   ```

2. After that, press *Tab* when the typing reaches `aleppo` (document real name contains Arabic characters, and unfortunately, Cuckoo Sandbox seems to *not* support Arabic characters so we need to rename it to `aleppo_plan_crecs.pdf`). In this case the document is located inside the `shares` folder. We have to change it based on where you put that document.

```
devil@TheDevilInside:~/Documents/cuckoo$ python utils/submit.py --platform windows --package pdf shares/aleppo_plan_cercs.pdf
Success: File "/home/devil/Documents/cuckoo/shares/aleppo_plan_cercs.pdf" added as task with ID 12
```

Please make sure you have a **Success** message with **task with ID 12**, as shown in the preceding screenshot. Cuckoo will then start taking the latest snapshot of the virtual machine that has been made. Windows will open the PDF document automatically.

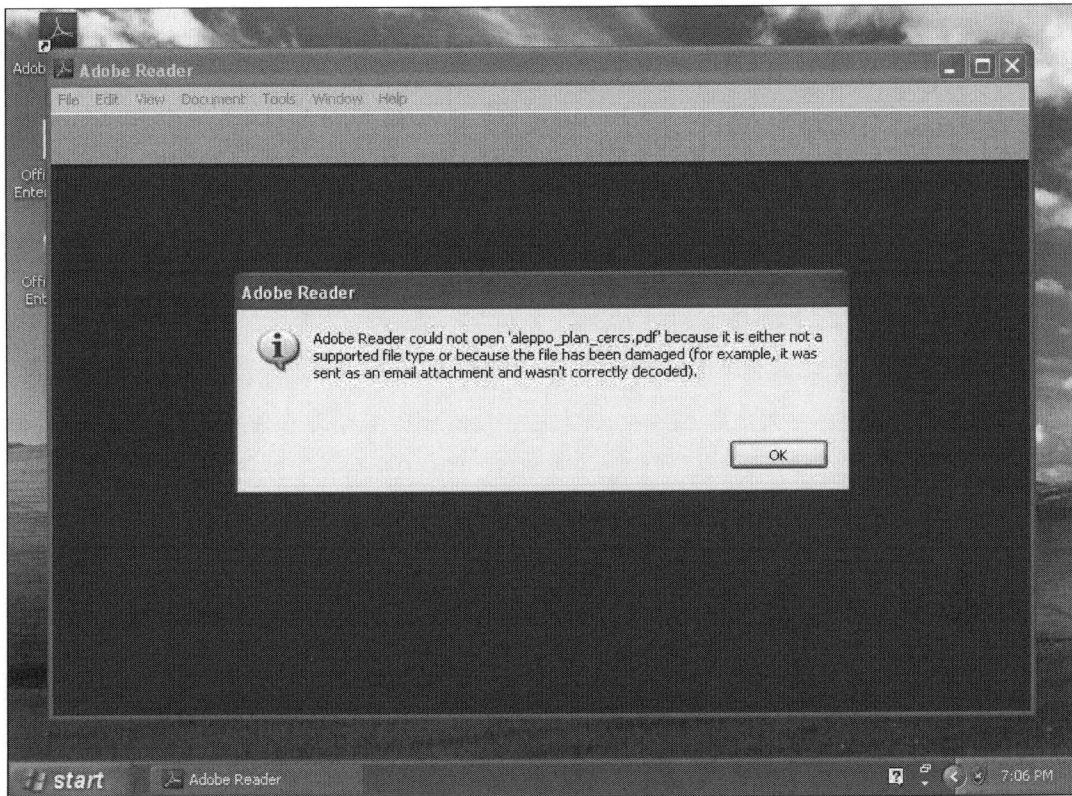

It seems that the document cannot be opened. You may want to know why.
The answer to this may be available at the Cuckoo report. Click on **OK** in the
information window. Wait a moment to make sure that Cuckoo can log all the
activities happening. Close Adobe Reader and wait until VM closes automatically.

After the VM has closed and task 12 (this task ID may be different in your OS) is finished, let's see the `report.html` file which is available at `storage/analyses/12`. Now, you can open the `report.html` file in your web browser.

Let's see the report in the **VirusTotal** section:

From the report of **VirusTotal**, we can see that the malware PDF is a Trojan. **McAfee** antivirus called this malware **Artemis!BC403BEF3C23**, while **ClamAV** seems to not recognize it. **Kaspersky** calls it by the name **Backdoor.Win32.DarkKomet.rzh**. Whatever the name is, it is concluded that the document may harm your computer by because it contains Trojan inside it.

Submitting a malware Excel document – CVE-2011-0609_XLS-SWF-2011-03-08_ crsenvironscan.xls

This section deals with spreadsheet documents that contain malware samples. Please make sure that you have installed the Microsoft Office bundled program in your VM environment. Internet connection in your VM environment is also needed to make sure that the malware analysis can run smoothly in your VM environment.

We will now submit an Excel file as the malware document. Let us see the steps involved:

1. Open a new **Terminal** tab (*Shift + Ctrl + T*) and type in the following command line:

    ```
    $ python utils/submit.py --platform windows --package xls
    shares/CVE-2011-0609_XLS-SWF-2011-03-08_crsenvironscan.xls
    ```

    ```
    devil@TheDevilInside:~/Documents/cuckoo$ python utils/submit.py --platform windows --package xls  shares/CVE-2011-0609_XLS-SWF-2011-03-08_crsenvironsc
    an.xls
    Success: File "/home/devil/Documents/cuckoo/shares/CVE-2011-0609_XLS-SWF-2011-03-08_crsenvironscan.xls" added as task with ID 13
    ```

    Please make sure you have a **Success** message, as shown in the preceding screenshot, with **task with ID 13**. Windows will open the Excel document.

2. Then let Cuckoo start the analysis process on the Guest OS:

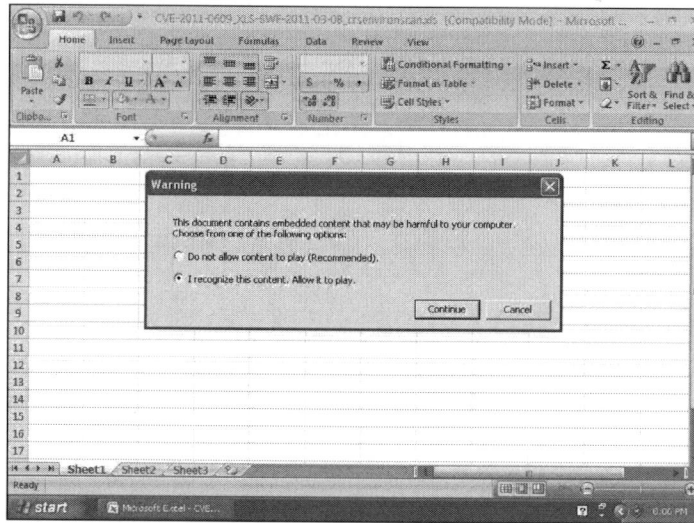

3. A warning pop-up window will appear. Again, we assume that the user didn't know what that warning was. So, we will choose **I recognize this content. Allow it to play**. and click on the **Continue** button. Wait a moment until the malware document takes some action. The VM will close automatically after all the actions are finished by the malware document.

4. Let's look at the subfolder of cuckoo located at `storage/analyses/13`.

5. Open the subfolder `reports`, and then open `report.html` in your web browser:

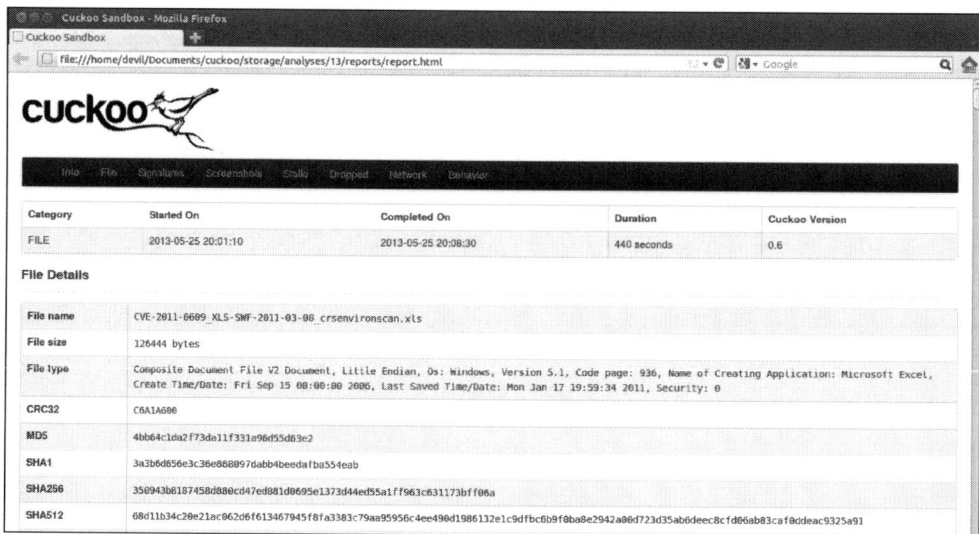

In the **VirusTotal** section, the malware was named as **Exploit-CVE2011-0609**.

6. From the **Dropped Files** tab, it seems that the malware uses Shockwave Flash objects to run the exploit code. No bug on the Excel file is used. This malware uses a Shockwave Flash bug that may be available on the victim's computer:

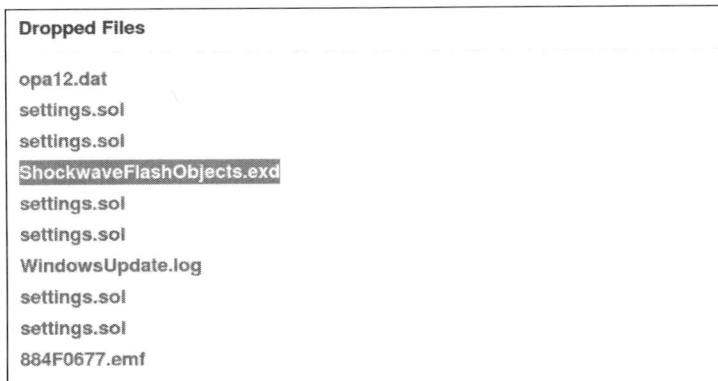

```
Dropped Files

opa12.dat
settings.sol
settings.sol
ShockwaveFlashObjects.exd
settings.sol
settings.sol
WindowsUpdate.log
settings.sol
settings.sol
884F0677.emf
```

Submitting a malicious URL – http://youtibe.com

This section deals with submitting a malicious URL for malware analysis. By default, the browser in the VM environment is Internet Explorer. You can use the default IE or another web browser. Do not forget to install a flash add-on in your browser. Internet connection in your VM environment is also needed to make sure that the malware analysis can run smoothly in your VM environment.

Since we will run a malicious URL, a network configuration change must be made. In *Chapter 1, Getting Started with Automated Malware Analysis using Cuckoo Sandbox*, we set the **Network** in our VM as **Host-only Adapter** to prevent the malware from making contact outside the Host. To submit a malware URL we must set the **Network** adapter in the Guest OS to connect to the Internet. To do it:

1. Make sure you have your VM turned off first.
2. Simply right-click on the VM and pick **Settings....** A new window will appear.

3. Select **Network**, tick the checkbox **Enable Network Adapter**, and from the **Attached to** drop-down menu, choose **Bridged Adapter**.

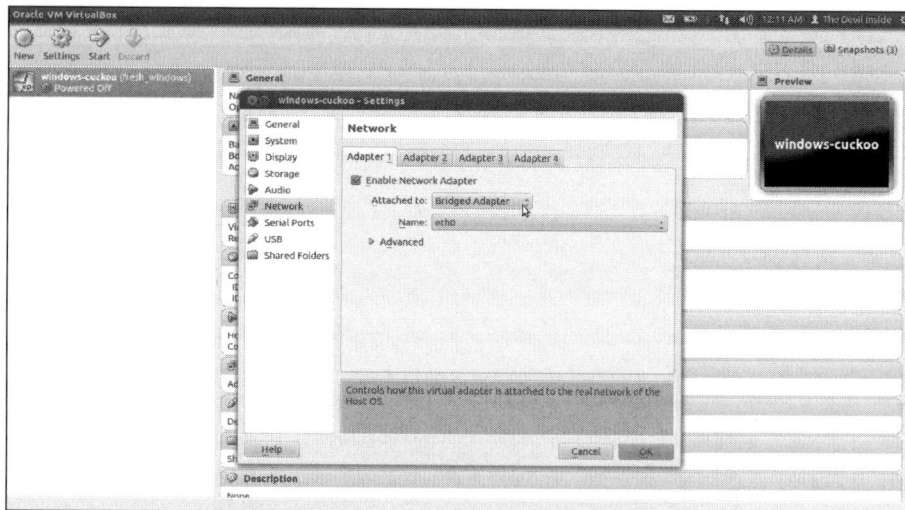

You can also disable the **Attached to Host-Only Adapter** (in my case Adapter 2 is the Host-only Adapter) and click on **OK**.

4. We should delete the previous adapter (**vboxnet0**) because the host machine may only know how to connect to the guest via that adapter. So when we have a network adapter attached to a bridge adapter, it will have a strange behavior. We can delete it by navigating to **File | Preferences...**. In the **Network** section, select the adapter and click on the second icon in the side panel that says **Remove host-only network (Del)** when we hover over it, then **OK**.

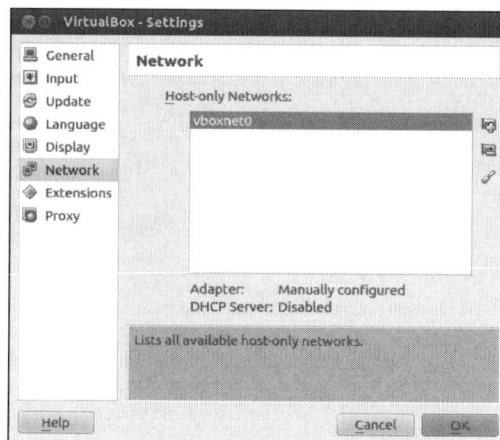

5. We need to power ON windows-cuckoo. There are some changes to be made in the Guest OS. After the booting process, go to Windows Start menu | **Control Panel** | **Network and Internet Connection** | **Network Connections**.

6. We will see a clickable option **Local Area Connection** there. Right-click on it and then click on **Properties**. Change the IP address and subnet mask by double-clicking on **Internet Protocol (TCP/IP)** to match your network segment (in this case, we change it to `192.168.2.102/24` which is a different IP).

7. Then fill the default gateway that matches your LAN connection so that the guest could later make a connection to the Internet.

8. Fill the **Preferred DNS Server** address as `8.8.8.8` (Google DNS) or whichever IP to be the DNS.

9. Take a snapshot then and turn it off.

10. Cuckoo configuration must be changed too. (Please see *Chapter 1, Getting Started with Automated Malware Analysis using Cuckoo Sandbox* for the explanation on how to change it.)

11. Make the change to `cuckoo.conf, interface = eth0` (because in bridge mode, the only physical interface available is `eth0`).

12. In the `virtualbox.conf` file, in the IP section, set it to your Guest's IP (in my case, the IP is 192.168.2.102).

13. Restart `cuckoo.py` and simply press *Ctrl + C* (if `cuckoo.py` is still running) and start it again with the command `python cuckoo.py`.

14. Close the browser or other applications that need Internet in the host machine, because it might hamper the report later.

   Now we are ready to submit the malware URL:

   ```
   $ python utils/submit.py --url http://www.youtibe.com
   ```

   Please note that the URL above may not be available by the time we try it. You can look for the reported malware URL in `malwaredomainlist.com/mdl.php` or other sites that provide malware URLs (you will find a lot of dead links so be patient). If you have found another suspicious malware URL, do not hesitate to submit it to Cuckoo to be analyzed.

   ```
   devil@TheDevilInside:~/Documents/cuckoo$ python utils/submit.py --url http://www.youtibe.com
   Success: URL "http://www.youtibe.com" added as task with ID 17
   ```

15. Make sure you have a **Success** message, as shown in the preceding screenshot with **task with ID 17**.

   Windows will open the URL in Internet Explorer.

16. We can see that we are redirected to some web pages simultaneously and end on a global marketing site which may be embedded with a fake flash player. The user may believe that it's youtube.com, but surely it will go to youtibe.com (only one character different).

We will finally land on a random advertising website. Annoying right?

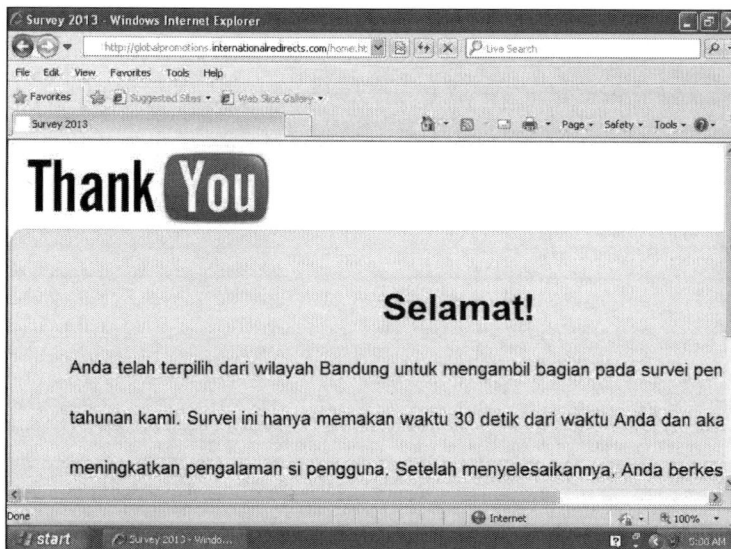

Submitting a malicious URL – http://ziti.cndesign.com/biaozi/fdc/page_07.htm

We will now submit a URL as a malware document. Let us see the steps involved:

1. Type in the following command:

```
$ python utils/submit.py --url
http://ziti.cndesign.com/biaozi/fdc/page_07.htm
```

> Please note that the URL above may not be available by the time we try it. You may look for the reported malware URL at http://www.scumware.org or another site that provides malware URL, or if we have found another suspicious malware URL we can submit it to Cuckoo to be analyzed.

```
devil@TheDevilInside:~/Documents/cuckoo$ python utils/submit.py --url http://ziti.cndesign.com/biaozi/fdc/page_07.htm
Success: URL "http://ziti.cndesign.com/biaozi/fdc/page_07.htm" added as task with ID 46
```

2. Please make sure you have a **Success** message as shown in the preceding screenshot with **task with ID 46**.

   Windows will open the URL with Internet Explorer.

3. When you open the URL you will find a web page containing a lot of design pictures. Nothing seems to be suspicious as of now:

4. Let's see the `report.html` file from Cuckoo Sandbox. Based on the ID, we will find it at `storage/analyses/46/reports`:

5. See on the **Dropped Files** section:

```
desktop.ini
00[1].gif
TN_cndesign1789[1].jpg
hy_r1_c6[1].jpg
autoexec.bat
D0F063B6B88A2B8BFE21C3993A613447
hy_r1_c1[1].jpg
TN_cndesign1741[1].jpg
```

There is **autoexec.bat** which is dropped when we were loading the web page. Now it seems suspicious. How come an ordinary web page could leave a **BAT file** (a type of script file, a text file containing a series of commands to be executed by the command interpreter). The scumware.org web page has a trojan called Troj/Fujif-Gen. Members of Troj/Fujif-Gen are usually clean files that have been modified to include an iframe pointing to remote malicious code. Maybe that's why this web page dropped a .bat file. But to make the right conclusion, we must do further analysis.

Submitting a binary file – Sality.G.exe

This section deals with binary files that contain malware samples. For this purpose, we may need to isolate the environment of the malware once again.

1. Please repeat adding the **Host-only Adapter** vboxnet0 and set it just the way we did in *Chapter 1, Getting Started with Automated Malware Analysis using Cuckoo Sandbox.*

2. Start the windows-cuckoo from VirtualBox, set the IP, and save the snapshot of it.

3. Remember to turn it off, change the Cuckoo configuration, and restart it.

4. You can start to analyze the binary file using the following command:

    ```
    $ python utils/submit.py --platform windows
    shares/Sality.G.exe
    ```

```
devil@TheDevilInside:~/Documents/cuckoo$ python utils/submit.py --platform windows shares/Sality.G.exe
Success: File "/home/devil/Documents/cuckoo/shares/Sality.G.exe" added as task with ID 50
```

5. Also remember that the .exe file was named as Sality.G.exe in order to warn the user that this file is a virus named Sality.G.exe. This file disguises itself as a keygen and activator for certain software.

6. Please make sure you have a **Success** message as shown in the preceding screenshot with **task with ID 50**.

   Windows will open the binary file.

7. We do not need to add the `--package` argument because the default package that Cuckoo will execute first contains `.exe` files. And actually we do not need to add the `- -platform windows` argument because by default we have configured it in `.conf` files. But just to make sure it works, as we hope for, we just add it.

   Windows will open the `.exe` file and a pop-up window will appear as shown in the following screenshot:

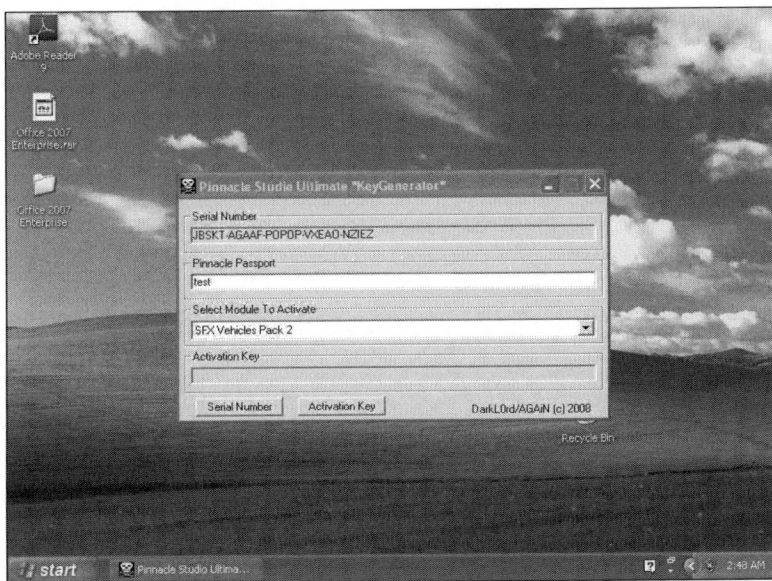

The malware binary disguises itself as a key generator for some software. The reason behind this is because people intend to have free software, so they must have this kind of software. They will not care whether some antivirus is warning them. It will run because people needed it the most.

Let's see the `report.html` from Cuckoo Sandbox. Based on the ID, we will find it at `storage/analyses/50/reports`.

Open the `report.html` in your web browser:

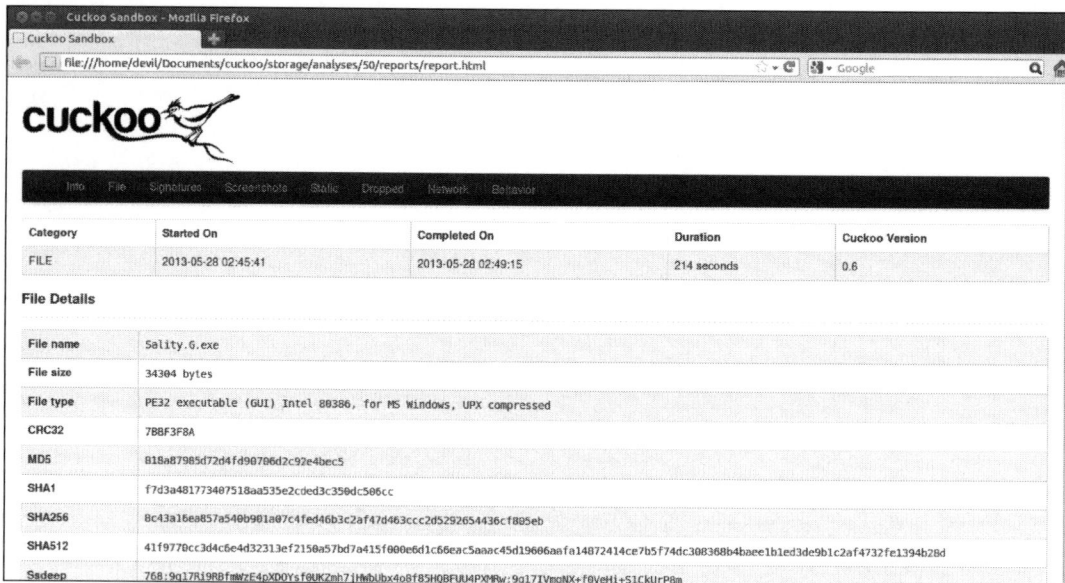

Please take a look at the **VirusTotal** section:

VirusTotal	38/42 (collapse)	
	Antivirus	**Result**
	nProtect	Win32.Sality.E
	CAT-QuickHeal	None
	K7AntiVirus	Virus
	TheHacker	W32/Sality(rp).I
	VirusBuster	Win32.Sality.L
	NOD32	Win32/Sality.NAE
	F-Prot	W32/Sality.K
	Symantec	W32.HLLP.Sality.O
	Norman	W32/Sality.N
	ByteHero	None
	TrendMicro-HouseCall	PE_SALITY.AE
	Avast	Win32:Sality-U
	eSafe	Win32.Sality.gen
	ClamAV	W32.Sality.N
	Kaspersky	Virus.Win32.Sality.I

That `.exe` file was identified as a virus named **Sality**. Now continue to the **Static Analysis** section:

Static Analysis

Sections

Name	Virtual Address	Virtual Size	Size of Raw Data	Entropy
UPX0	0x1000	0x8000	0x0	0.0
UPX1	0x9000	0x3000	0x2c00	7.7689419641
.rsrc	0xc000	0x1000	0x600	2.0024153352
.NUPX1	0xd000	0x5000	0x5000	7.9814521051

Imports

```
Library KERNEL32.DLL:
 • 0x40c428 - LoadLibraryA
 • 0x40c42c - GetProcAddress
 • 0x40c430 - VirtualProtect
 • 0x40c434 - VirtualAlloc
 • 0x40c438 - VirtualFree
 • 0x40c43c - ExitProcess
```

It will import some library form `KERNEL32.DLL`.

```
Registry Keys
 • HKEY_LOCAL_MACHINE\Software\Microsoft\Windows NT\CurrentVersion\IMM
 • HKEY_CURRENT_USER\SOFTWARE\Microsoft\CTF
 • HKEY_LOCAL_MACHINE\Software\Microsoft\CTF\SystemShared
 • HKEY_LOCAL_MACHINE\SOFTWARE\Microsoft\Windows NT\CurrentVersion\LanguagePack\SurrogateFallback
 • HKEY_LOCAL_MACHINE\Software\Microsoft\Windows\CurrentVersion\Run
 • HKEY_CURRENT_USER\Keyboard Layout\Toggle
 • HKEY_CURRENT_USER\SOFTWARE\Microsoft\CTF\LangBarAddIn\
 • HKEY_LOCAL_MACHINE\SOFTWARE\Microsoft\CTF\LangBarAddIn\
 • HKEY_CURRENT_USER\Software\Microsoft\Windows\CurrentVersion\Run
```

The malware binary then will access and put some entry into the registry. As you may see, it will access the registry entry, such as `HKEY_LOCAL_MACHINE\Software\Microsoft\Windows\CurrentVersion\Run` that defines the programs that can run at startup. This is typical of common virus activity to maintain their access to the victim's computer.

Now let's see what the virus is doing in the host machine in detail. In the **Processes** section, we will see an entry like the following screenshot:

Processes

    registry   filesystem   process   services   network   synchronization

Sality.G.exe PID: 1108, Parent PID: 188

Click on **Sality.G.exe** and we will see its details in the following screenshot:

02:47:11,230	1344	NtCreateFile	FileHandle => 0x00000074 DesiredAccess => 0x40100080 FileName => C:\WINDOWS \system32\wmimgr32.dl_ CreateDisposition => 5 ShareAccess => 1	SUCCESS	0x00000000
02:47:11,230	1344	NtWriteFile	FileHandle => 0x00000074 Buffer =>	SUCCESS	0x00000000
02:47:11,240	1344	NtOpenKey	KeyHandle => 0x00000074 DesiredAccess => 1 ObjectAttributes => Registry\MACHINE \System \CurrentControlSet \Control\Session Manager	SUCCESS	0x00000000
02:47:11,240	1344	NtQueryValueKey	KeyHandle => 0x00000074 ValueName => SafeProcessSearchMode	FAILURE	3221225524
02:47:11,240	1344	NtCreateFile	FileHandle => 0x00000074 DesiredAccess => 0x80100080 FileName => C:\WINDOWS \system32\wmimgr32.dl_ CreateDisposition => 1 ShareAccess => 3	SUCCESS	0x00000000

As we can see , the binary malware tried to make a file in C:\WINDOWS\system32\. A lot of activities like that may occur as you may have seen in the report.

> More about utils option can be found in this page:
> (https://cuckoo.readthedocs.org/en/latest/usage/utilities.html)
>
> If you want to repeat the above process. Just use the following command:
> ```
> $ python utils/process.py [task ID]
> ```
> For example, you may use command:
> ```
> $ python utils/process.py 50
> ```
> From this example, you are running again the process engine for analysis number 50.
>
> Or, if you just want to re-generate the report please use command:
> ```
> $ python utils/process.py --report [task ID]
> ```

Memory forensic using Cuckoo Sandbox – using memory dump features

This section deals with memory forensic using **Volatility**. This chapter only introduces a little bit about the Volatility feature and its installation. Detailed explanation and exercises will be provided in the next chapter. This section will guide you on how to install Volatility and its basic usage.

Now we are ready to use more advanced Cuckoo features. It was Cuckoo's ability to take a memory dump of running processes in the Guest OS. First, we need to modify the configuration for Cuckoo so that the memory dump may be created before the machine shuts down:

1. Edit the `cuckoo.conf` file that is in the `conf/` directory and write down the configuration `memory_dump` = `on`.

2. Edit the `reporting.conf` file in the same directory `conf/` and activate `metadata` and `maec11`:

    ```
    [metadata]
    enabled = on

    [maec11]
    enabled = on
    ```

3. Save it.

Please only enable them when you think you need further analysis to the memory that the malware used, because it will make your analysis files grow larger. If Cuckoo has started, press *Ctrl* + *C* to stop it, and then start it again.

We will submit a binary file for the analysis using the memory dump feature of Cuckoo:

1. Type in the following command:

    ```
    $ python utils/submit.py --platform windows
    shares/SwInit_Virut.exe
    ```

    Remember that the `.exe` file was named `SwInit_Virut.exe` in order to inform you that this file was a virus named `Virut`.

    ```
    devil@TheDevilInside:~/Documents/cuckoo$ python utils/submit.py --platform windows shares/SwInit_Virut.exe
    Success: File "/home/devil/Documents/cuckoo/shares/SwInit_Virut.exe" added as task with ID 51
    ```

2. Make sure you get a **Success** message, as shown in the preceding screenshot with **task with ID 51**.

    Windows will open the binary file.

3. When the malware file is opened by the Guest OS, nothing happens on the windows GUI. But in the background process, who knows, something might happen.

4. Go to the directory `storage/analyses/51/`. There is a memory dump file named `memory.dmp`. The file size is about 822.7 MB! This is why we must use this option only when we need further analysis.

As usual, please see the generated `report.html` in reports folder:

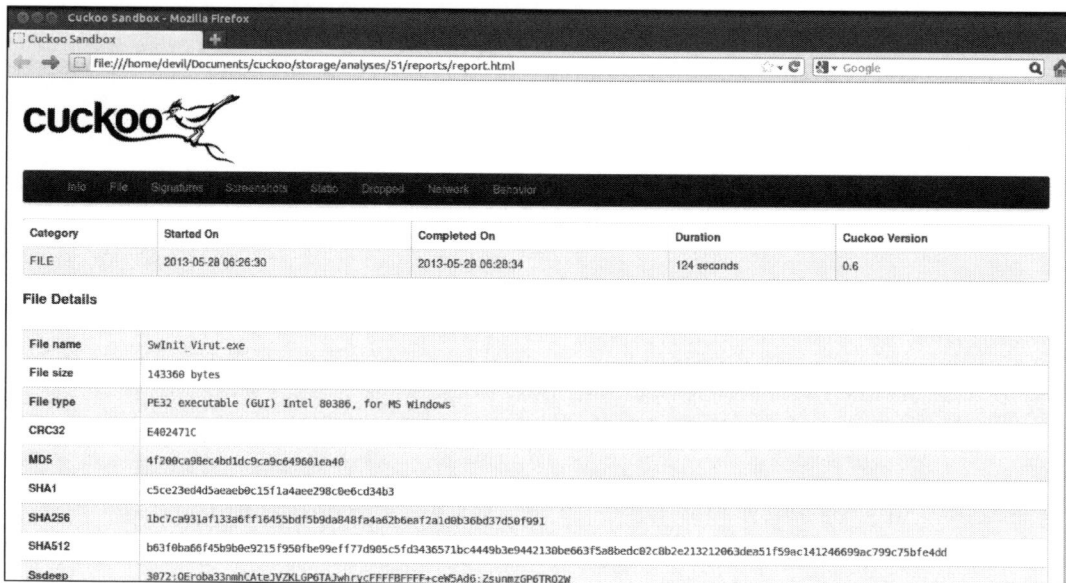

Yara has now confirmed that this file contains **shellcode**. In the **VirusTotal** section, you may see the malware was named by **W32.Virut**:

Yara	• shellcode (Matched shellcode byte patterns)	
VirusTotal	37/46 (collapse)	
	Antivirus	**Result**
	MicroWorld-eScan	None
	nProtect	None
	CAT-QuickHeal	W32.Virut.G
	McAfee	W32/Virut.n.gen
	Malwarebytes	None
	K7AntiVirus	Virus
	K7GW	Virus
	TheHacker	None
	NANO-Antivirus	Virus.Win32.Virut.hpeg
	F-Prot	W32/Virut.AL!Generic
	Symantec	W32.Virut.CF
	Norman	Virut.HL
	TotalDefense	Win32/Virut.17408
	TrendMicro-HouseCall	PE_VIRUX.R

While performing static analysis with the help of Cuckoo, we may know that this virus tries to imitate legal software from Adobe Systems, which will look like a product of Adobe Shockwave Version 11.0 if users try to confirm its file version.

Static Analysis	
Version Infos	
LegalCopyright:	Copyright \xa9 1985-2008 Adobe Systems, Inc.
InternalName:	SwInit
FileVersion:	11.0r458
CompanyName:	Adobe Systems, Inc.
LegalTrademarks:	Director\xae is a registered trademark and Shockwave(tm) is a trademark of Adobe Systems, Inc.
ProductName:	Shockwave
ProductVersion:	11.0
FileDescription:	Shockwave Init
OriginalFilename:	SwInit.exe
LegalCopyright:	Copyright \xa9 1985-2008 Adobe Systems, Inc.
InternalName:	SwInit
FileVersion:	11.0r458
CompanyName:	Adobe Systems, Inc.
LegalTrademarks:	Director\xae is a registered trademark and Shockwave(tm) is a trademark of Adobe Systems, Inc.
ProductName:	Shockwave

In the **Processes** section, you may find the malware's activities. In the following screenshot, you can see that it will write a registry and take action as if it were a real Shockwave 11. Let's take a look at the value of `RegCreateKeyExA`:

06:28:06,393	244	RegCreateKeyExA	Registry => 0x80000001 SubKey => Software\Adobe \Shockwave 11 Class => Access => 983103 Handle => 0x0000008c	SUCCESS	0x00000000
06:28:06,393	244	RegCreateKeyExW	Registry => 0x0000008c SubKey => swstate Class => Access => 983103 Handle => 0x00000088	SUCCESS	0x00000000
06:28:06,393	244	RegOpenKeyExA	Registry => 0x00000088 SubKey => Handle => 0x00000090	SUCCESS	0x00000000
06:28:06,393	244	RegCloseKey	Handle => 0x00000088	SUCCESS	0x00000000
06:28:06,393	244	RegSetValueExW	Handle => 0x00000090 ValueName => Type => 1 Buffer => 0\x00	SUCCESS	0x00000000
06:28:06,393	244	RegCloseKey	Handle => 0x00000090	SUCCESS	0x00000000
06:28:06,393	244	RegCloseKey	Handle => 0x0000008c	SUCCESS	0x00000000

Additional memory forensic using Volatility

Now after we dump the memory, we need to do some forensics on it. The tool we will use is called **Volatility Framework**. It can extract digital artifacts from volatile memory (RAM) dumps. Volatility can analyze RAM dumps from 32-bit and 64-bit Windows, Linux, Mac OS, and Android systems.

1. Download the latest Volatility available.

2. After you finish downloading the file, you have to extract the files into a folder:

   ```
   $ tar -zxvf volatility-2.2.tar.gz
   ```

   > Find the latest Volatility download link here: https://code.
   > google.com/p/volatility/wiki/VolatilityIntroduction

3. Change the directory to `volatility-2.2`:

   ```
   $ cd volatility-2.2/
   $ ls
   ```

   Our memory analysis will be using the `vol.py` file.

   > For a detailed documentation about using Volatility, please see the following Wikipedia links:
   >
   > https://code.google.com/p/volatility/wiki/Release22
   >
   > https://code.google.com/p/volatility/wiki/CommandReference22
   >
   > https://code.google.com/p/volatility/wiki/VolatilityUsage22

Using Volatility

Let us see the steps involved while using Volatility:

1. Show the image information of memory.dmp:

   ```
   $ python vol.py -f
   ../cuckoo/storage/analyses/51/memory.dmpimageinfo
   ```

   ```
   devil@TheDevilInside:~/Documents/volatility-2.2$ python vol.py -f ../cuckoo/storage/analyses/51/memory.dmp imageinfo
   Volatile Systems Volatility Framework 2.2
   Determining profile based on KDBG search...

           Suggested Profile(s) : WinXPSP2x86, WinXPSP3x86 (Instantiated with WinXPSP2x86)
                      AS Layer1 : FileAddressSpace (/home/devil/Documents/cuckoo/storage/analyses/51/memory.dmp)
                       PAE type : No PAE
                            DTB : 0x39000L
                           KDBG : 0x54d5d0
           Number of Processors : 0
      Image Type (Service Pack) : -
              KUSER_SHARED_DATA : 0xffdf0000L
   devil@TheDevilInside:~/Documents/volatility-2.2$
   ```

2. Show the KDBG structures information:

   ```
   $ python vol.py -f ../cuckoo/storage/analyses/51/memory.dmp --
   profile=WinXPSP3x86 kdbgscan
   ```

   ```
   devil@TheDevilInside:~/Documents/volatility-2.2$ python vol.py -f ../cuckoo/storage/analyses/51/memory.dmp --profile=WinXPSP3x86 kdbgscan
   Volatile Systems Volatility Framework 2.2
   **************************************************
   Instantiating KDBG using: /home/devil/Documents/cuckoo/storage/analyses/51/memory.dmp WinXPSP3x86 (5.1.0 32bit)
   Offset (P)                    : 0x54d5d0
   KDBG owner tag check          : True
   Profile suggestion (KDBGHeader): WinXPSP3x86
   Version64                     : 0x54d5a8 (Major: 15, Minor: 2600)
   PsActiveProcessHead           : 0x80561458
   PsLoadedModuleList            : 0x8055b2c0
   KernelBase                    : 0x804d7000

   **************************************************
   Instantiating KDBG using: /home/devil/Documents/cuckoo/storage/analyses/51/memory.dmp WinXPSP3x86 (5.1.0 32bit)
   Offset (P)                    : 0x54d5d0
   KDBG owner tag check          : True
   Profile suggestion (KDBGHeader): WinXPSP2x86
   Version64                     : 0x54d5a8 (Major: 15, Minor: 2600)
   PsActiveProcessHead           : 0x80561458
   PsLoadedModuleList            : 0x8055b2c0
   KernelBase                    : 0x804d7000
   ```

   We can choose this option from many OS profiles, for example:

   - Win2003SP2x64: A Profile for Windows 2003 SP2 x64
   - Win2003SP2x86: A Profile for Windows 2003 SP2 x86
   - Win2008SP2x64: A Profile for Windows 2008 SP2 x64
   - Win2008SP2x86: A Profile for Windows 2008 SP2 x86
   - Win7SP1x64: A Profile for Windows 7 SP1 x64
   - Win7SP1x86: A Profile for Windows 7 SP1 x86
   - WinXPSP2x86: A Profile for Windows XP SP2 x86
   - WinXPSP3x86: A Profile for Windows XP SP3 x86

> The complete list of the supported profile can be seen here:
> `https://code.google.com/p/volatility/wiki/VolatilityU`
> `sage22#Selecting_a_Profile`

Summary

In this chapter, you have learned how to submit malware samples to Cuckoo Sandbox. This chapter also described multiple examples of the submission of malicious files that consist of MS Office documents, PDF files, binary files, and malicious URLs. In addition, this chapter also describes how to use Volatility as a memory forensic tool as part of additional tools in Cuckoo Sandbox. With volatility, you can analyze RAM dumps from 32-bit and 64-bit Windows, Linux, Mac OS, and Android systems. You just need to set up the profile before performing a memory forensic using Volatility. For example, if you want to perform memory forensics using Volatility for Windows XP, you need to change the Volatility profile using the Windows XP profile.

In the next chapter, we will explain in detail about the usage of Volatility and some examples of cases that will sharpen your knowledge about Volatilty as a memory forensic tool.

3
Analyzing the Output of Cuckoo Sandbox

In this chapter, we will discuss how to read the analysis output which was explained in the previous chapter. We will also discuss about **APT1 attack** (I think you must be familiar with the term APT1, which is recently being discussed quite often). If you have never heard of it you should read the *Advanced Persistent Threat (APT) and Insider Threat* blog post at `http://cyber-defense.sans.org/blog/2012/10/23/ advanced-persistent-threat-apt-and-insider-threat`. One of the discussions about APT is written by Mandiant, an IT security researching company. The released paper was a shocking report about APT1 attacks. In this report, Mandiant explained about a number of sophisticated malware that were being used for a few targeted companies or organizations. These kinds of malware not only steal data, but also spy on the activities of our daily life. We will try to analyze some sample APT1 malware that was used in the attack using Cuckoo Sandbox, and we will find out what kind of activities emerge from the malware.

I got some malware samples from repositories such as `VirusShare.com` and famous blogger Mila Parkour (`http://contagiodump.blogspot.com`). You need to download these malware samples, but of course, do it at your own risk or at least use a controlled virtual environment, and still be careful as we do not know what will happen if we are executing this malware.

We will use additional tools in this chapter — Wireshark, Yara, Radare, Bokken, and Volatility should be installed on your system to enhance the analysis process. You can find these software right here:

No.	Name	Download Links
1	Wireshark	`https://www.wireshark.org/download.html`
2	Yara	`http://code.google.com/p/yara-project/`
3	Radare	`http://radare.org/y/`
4	Bokken	`http://inguma.eu/projects/bokken`
5	Volatility	`https://volatility.googlecode.com/files/` `volatility-2.2.tar.gz`

The processing module

This is a script that describes custom ways of processing the analysis result from Cuckoo Sandbox. You can create a custom processing module. By default, processing modules in Cuckoo Sandbox are as follows:

- **AnalysisInfo** (`modules/processing/analysisinfo.py`): This module generates some basic information on the current analysis, such as timestamps, Version of Cuckoo, and so on

- **BehaviorAnalysis** (`modules/processing/behavior.py`): This module parses the raw behavioral logs and performs some initial trasnformations and interpretations, including the complete processes tracing, a behavioral summary, and a process tree

- **Debug** (`modules/processing/debug.py`): This module includes errors and the `analysis.log` generated by the analyzer

- **Dropped** (`modules/processing/dropped.py`): This module includes information on the files dropped by the malware and dumped by Cuckoo

- **NetworkAnalysis** (`modules/processing/network.py`): This module parses the PCAP files and extracts network information, such as DNS traffic, domains, IP addresses, HTTP requests, IRC, and SMTP traffic

- **StaticAnalysis** (`modules/processing/static.py`): This module performs some static analysis on PE32 files

- **Strings** (`modules/processing/static.py`): This module extracts strings from the analyzer binary
- **TargetInfo** (`modules/processing/targetinfo.py`): This module includes information, such as hashes, on the analyzed file
- **VirusTotal** (`modules/processing/virustotal.py`): Look up `virustotal.com` for AntiVirus signatures of the analyzed file

> The file is not uploaded on `virustotal.com`. If the file was not previously uploaded on the website no results will be retrieved.

In the previous chapter, we learned how to read the analysis from the output processing module.

Analyzing an APT attack using Cuckoo Sandbox, Volatility, and Yara

If you have not installed Volatility yet, carry out the following steps:

1. You can use this command to install the latest version of Volatility on your system:

   ```
   $ svn checkout http://volatility.googlecode.com/svn/trunk/
   volatility-
   read-only
   $ cd volatility-read-only
   $ python setup.py build
   $ sudo python setup.py install
   ```

2. To make things easier, you can make a shortcut alias command for Volatility by editing your `.bashrc` file:

   ```
   $ nano  ~/.bashrc
   ```

3. Go to the end of line, and add this command:

   ```
   $ alias vol.py="/home/user/Download/Volatility-read-
   only/vol.py
   ```

4. Save and Exit.

5. Please notice that `/home/user/Download/Volatility-read-only/vol.py` is the Volatility directory in your system.

    You can replace the line based on your Volatility folder in your system. Now, you can run Volatility by just typing this command in the terminal:

    ```
    $ vol.py
    ```

    Before continuing to analyze APT1 malware sample, you have to change some default configuration in your Cuckoo Sandbox.

6. Edit file `/cuckoo/conf/cuckoo.conf` using the following command line:

    ```
    $ nano cuckoo/conf/cuckoo.conf
    ```

7. Make sure that `memory_dump` is turned on (by default `memory_dump` is set as `off`) and again check your hard drive space because it will consume a large part of it. It will take the size of the virtual machine RAM:

    ```
    memory_dump = on
    ```

8. Edit file `/cuckoo/conf/reporting.conf`

    Change the default value of `[metadata]` and `[maec11]` to on (By default these are set as `off`)

    ```
    [metadata]
    enabled = on

    [maec11]
    enabled = on
    ```

9. Alienvault Labs create a Yara rule for APT1 attack. You have to download this rule first from the following URL:

    ```
    https://github.com/jaimeblasco/AlienvaultLabs/blob/master/
    malware_analysis/CommentCrew/apt1.yara
    ```

10. Rename the file to `apt1.yar` and save the rule in the `/cuckoo/data/yara` folder.

    You can see the APT1 rule in the following screenshot:

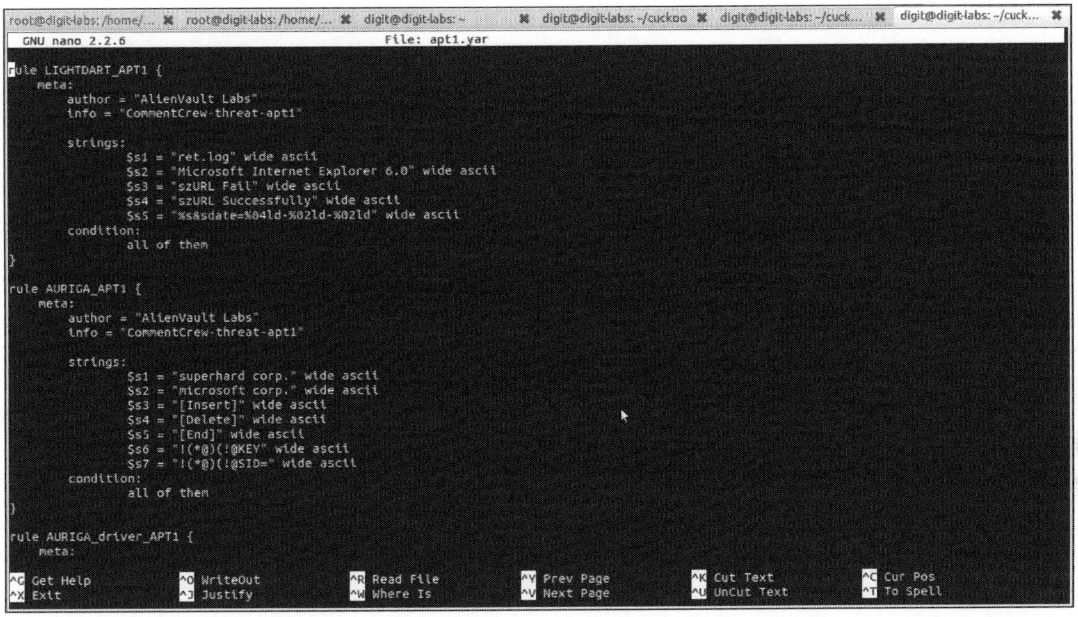

root@digit-labs: /home/...
root@digit-labs: /home/...
digit@digit-labs: ~
digit@digit-labs: ~/cuckoo
digit@digit-labs: ~/cuck...
digit@digit-labs: ~/cuck...
GNU nano 2.2.6
File: apt1.yar
rule LIGHTDART_APT1 {
meta:
author = "AlienVault Labs"
info = "CommentCrew-threat-apt1"
strings:
$s1 = "ret.log" wide ascii
$s2 = "Microsoft Internet Explorer 6.0" wide ascii
$s3 = "szURL Fail" wide ascii
$s4 = "szURL Successfully" wide ascii
$s5 = "%s&sdate=%04ld-%02ld-%02ld" wide ascii
condition:
all of them
}
rule AURIGA_APT1 {
meta:
author = "AlienVault Labs"
info = "CommentCrew-threat-apt1"
strings:
$s1 = "superhard corp." wide ascii
$s2 = "microsoft corp." wide ascii
$s3 = "[Insert]" wide ascii
$s4 = "[Delete]" wide ascii
$s5 = "[End]" wide ascii
$s6 = "!(*@)(!@KEY" wide ascii
$s7 = "!(*@)(!@SID=" wide ascii
condition:
all of them
}
rule AURIGA_driver_APT1 {
meta:
^G Get Help
^O WriteOut
^R Read File
^Y Prev Page
^K Cut Text
^C Cur Pos
^X Exit
^J Justify
^W Where Is
^V Next Page
^U UnCut Text
^T To Spell

11. Do not forget to add `apt1.yar` to the `index.yar` file. (Every time you add new Yara rules, you should add the rules in `index.yar` file.):

    `$ nano /cuckoo/data/yara/index.yar`

12. Add this parameter at the end of the Yara configuration file, as shown in the following screenshot:

```
include "apt1.yar"
```

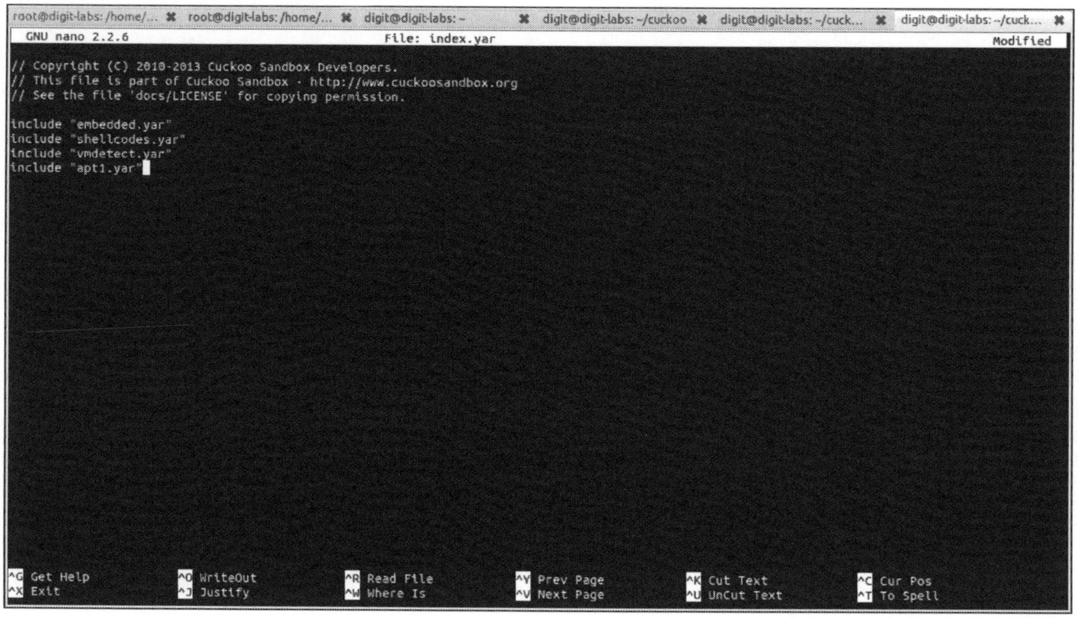

Save it and the APT1 Yara rule is ready to use. With this, we can check the file type of the malware samples, and also the string combination inside the malware sample. For an example we can use the following command line:

```
$ strings path/to/file/VirusShare_fc1937c1aa536b3744ebdfb1716fd54d |
egrep '.{6,}' | less
```

We need to use the disassembler application to view the executable files of the malware such as **Radare**. Radare is a reverse engineering framework that is widely used in disassembling, debugging, analyzing, and manipulating binary files.

And to make it even easier, we need a frontend application, **Bokken**. Bokken can use Radare or **Pyew** as a backend. A combination of Radare and Bokken can replace **IDA Pro** or other similar commercial tools that run on Linux. You need to install Radare, Bokken, and Pyew from the Ubuntu repository:

```
$ sudo apt-get install radare radare2 bokken pyew
```

After the installation process is completed, you can run Bokken from the unity dashboard or simply type the following command line in the terminal:

```
$ bokken
```

When Bokken is started, we can choose Radare or Pyew as the backend in BokkenOption. Now let's choose the malware sample that we want to analyze, as in the following screenshot:

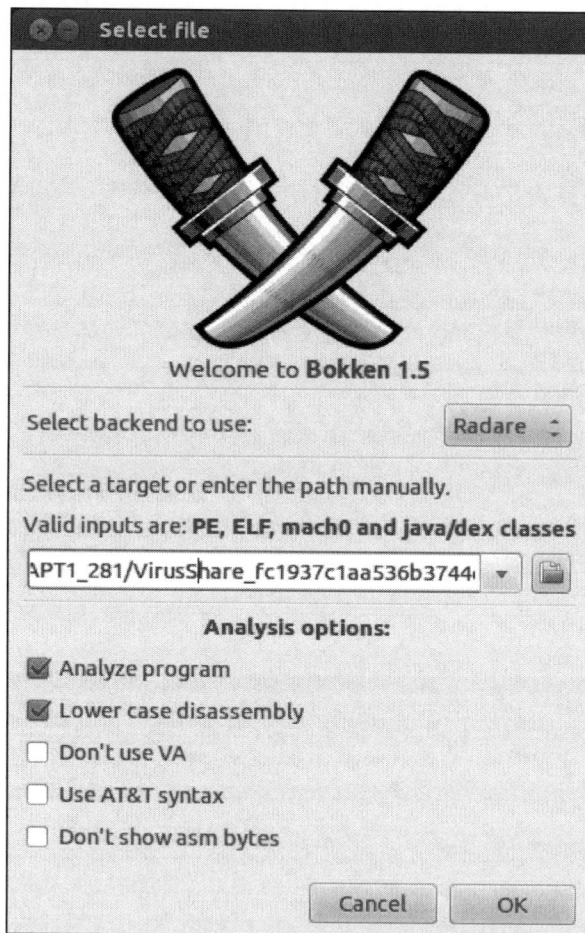

Bokken will start disassembling the binary file. In the first appearance, Bokken will show you the **Flowgraph** from the binary files, as shown in the following screenshot:

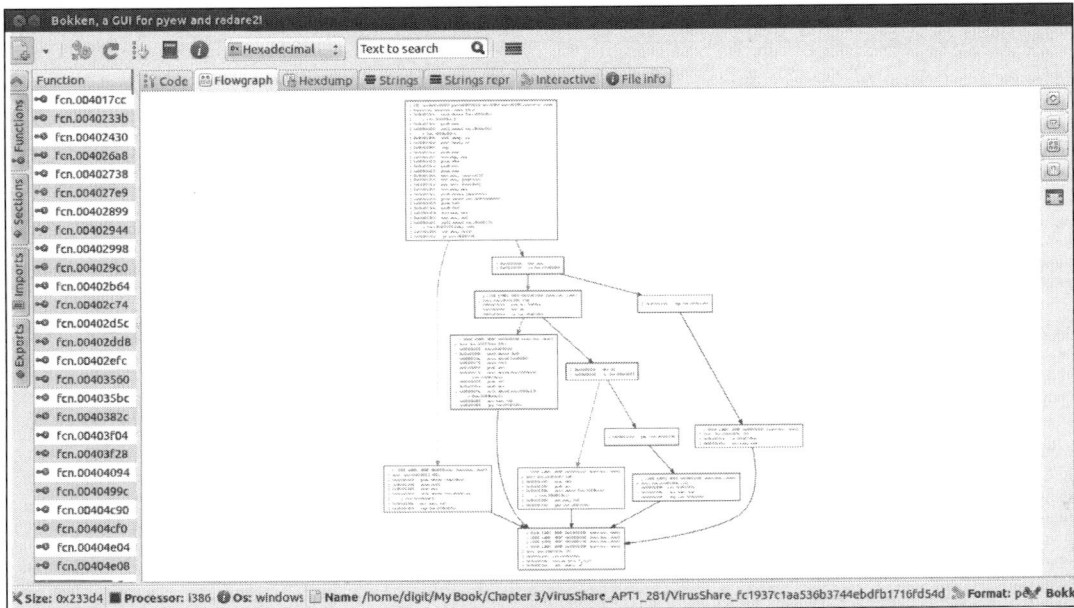

Beside the **Flowgraph** tab, we can also see the **Hexdump** tab in Bokken, as shown in the following screenshot:

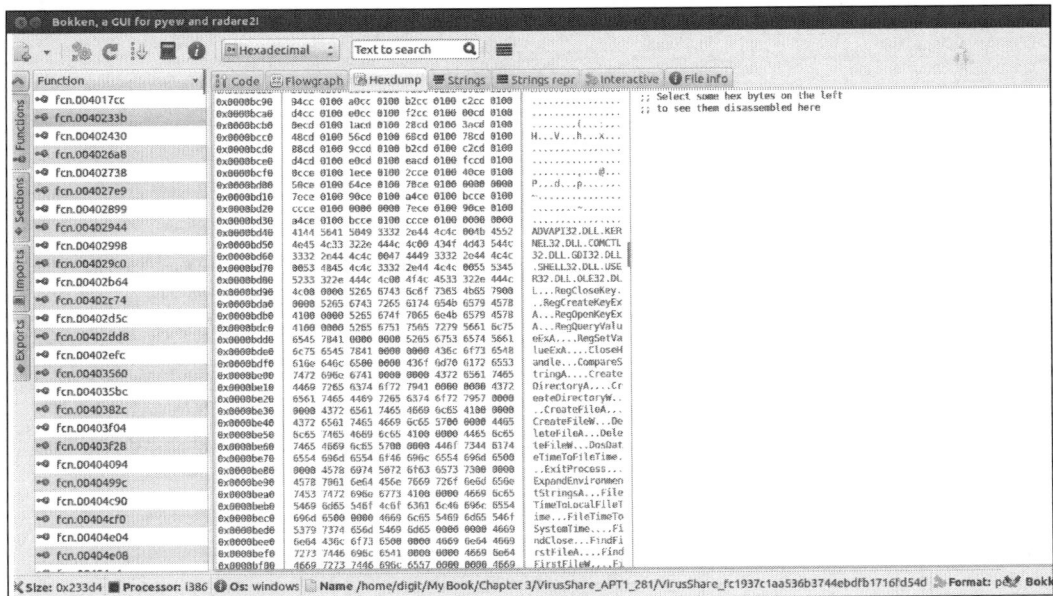

A brief explanation about the binary file can be found under the **File info** tab, as shown in the screenshot below:

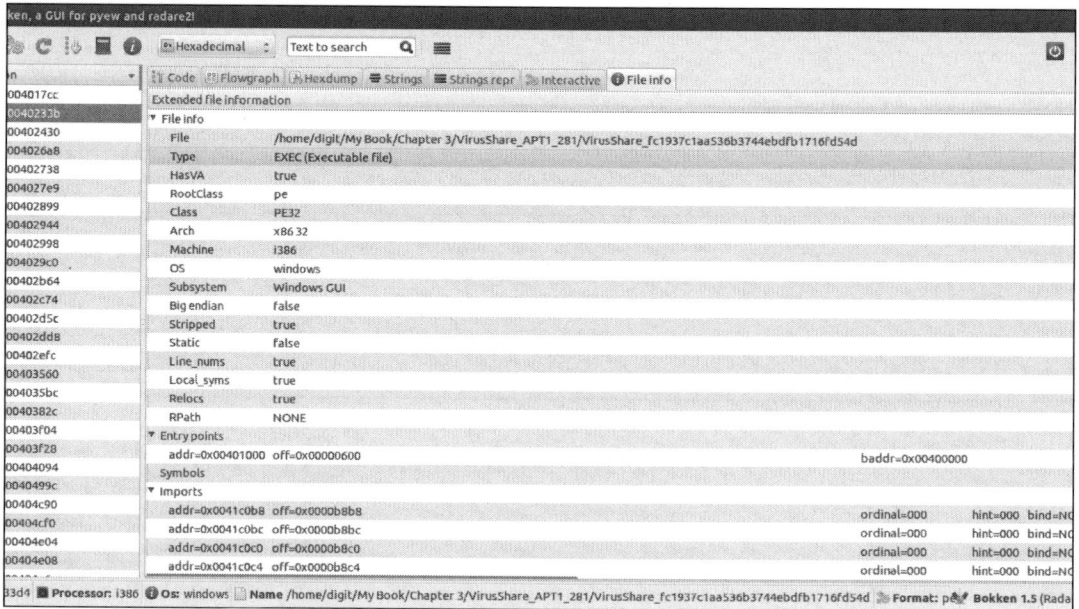

After playing with Radare and Bokken, now let's start the analysis process with Cuckoo Sandbox. We will use web-based Cuckoo Sandbox to analyze the sample malware:

1. Start your `cuckoo.py` and your `web.py`:

   ```
   $ ./cuckoo.py
   ```

   ```
   $ ./utils/web.py
   ```

2. Choose the binary malicious file that you want to analyze in the Cuckoo web interface and then click on **Submit** to upload the file.

Let's wait while Cuckoo Sandbox is analyzing the malware sample. During the analysis process, the Guest OS—Windows XP—will display a document entitled **Top Stock Alerts for Day Traders Facebook...**, as shown in the following screenshot:

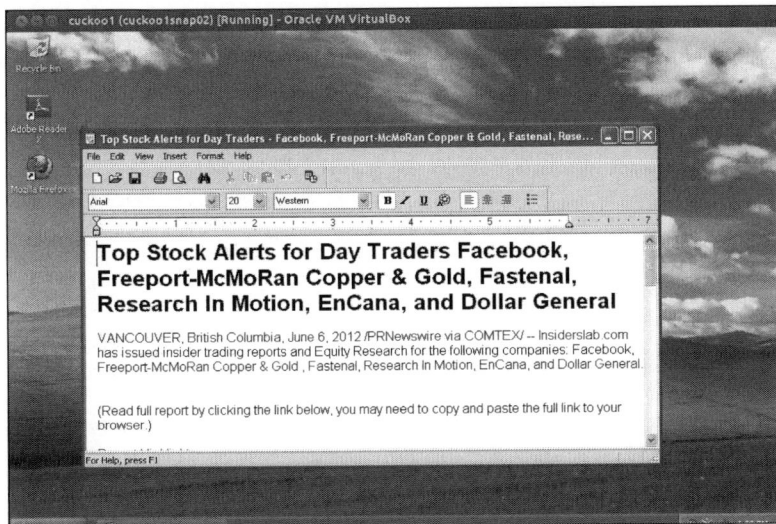

After the analyzing process is finished, we can browse the analysis result based on the task ID that was given when you submitted the binary sample, as shown in the following screenshot:

As we can see in the following screenshot, **Yara** detects the binary file as a **shellcode**:

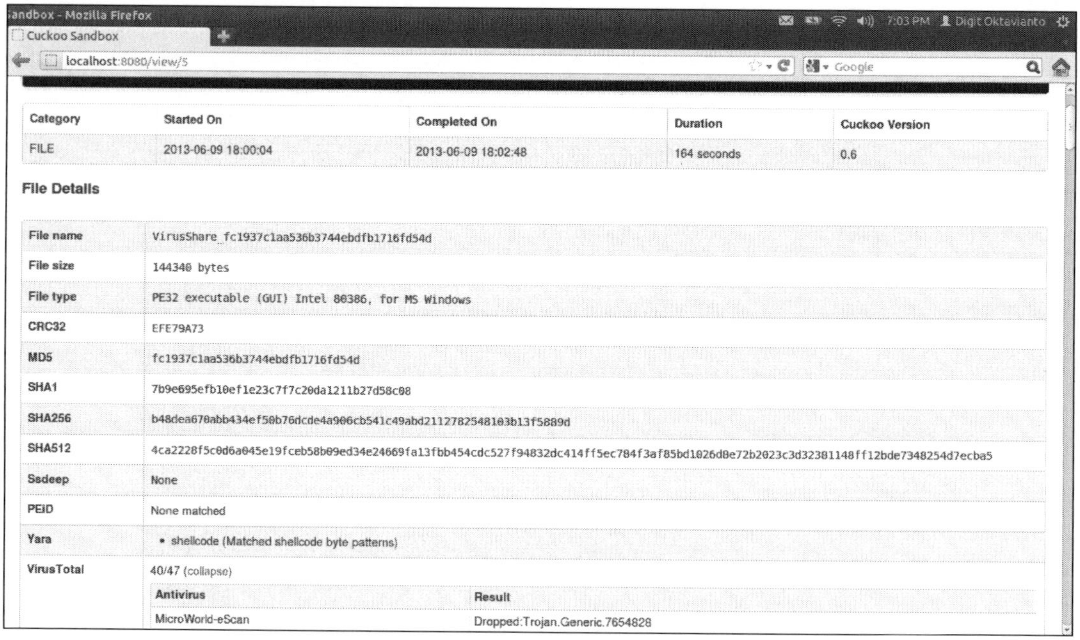

In case you are not familiar with shellcode, according to the book *Introduction to Shellcoding* by Michel Blomgren at `rootsecure.net`, **shellcode** is a piece of machine-readable code, or script code that has just one mission, to open up a command interpreter (shell) on the target system so that an "attacker" can type in commands in the same fashion as a regular authorized user, or system administrator of that system, does (with a few not-so-important exceptions of course).

For a malware, there are many types of shellcodes. Usually it is harder for us to detect because it is encoded. But, luckily, we have Yara to detect it for us. Although some new or customized shellcode will bypass it, at least we can identify most of it automatically with Cuckoo Sandbox.

If we pay attention to the results from a Yara signature, it indicates that there is something wrong with the binary file. Let's do a further analysis in this case.

As we can see in the preceding screenshot, **VirusTotal** analysis shows **40/47** antivirus detected the binary file as a malicious program. You can see the different name/version that was given by each antivirus. Because it is based on the malware classification from each vendor, they have their own codename for each malware.

Most antivirus vendors labeled the binary file as **Trojan-Downloader**; is it because of the malware activity that download mysterious files in every host that was infected by them?

Interesting case, but we have to analyze the behavior before reaching a conclusion. This is where the dynamic analysis plays its part in giving details about what the malware was doing in the infected system. Right from the beginning, when the malware was deployed in the system, what changes did it make in the system, and so on.

As long as the analysis is working, Cuckoo Sandbox will keep capturing all of the malware activities. If the analysis time is not long enough, the malware that are not immediately running while infecting the system will not be detected by Cuckoo Sandbox. It depends on us as malware analysts to adapt to this kind of situation by learning as much as we can, and gain more experience so that we know what to do in such situations.

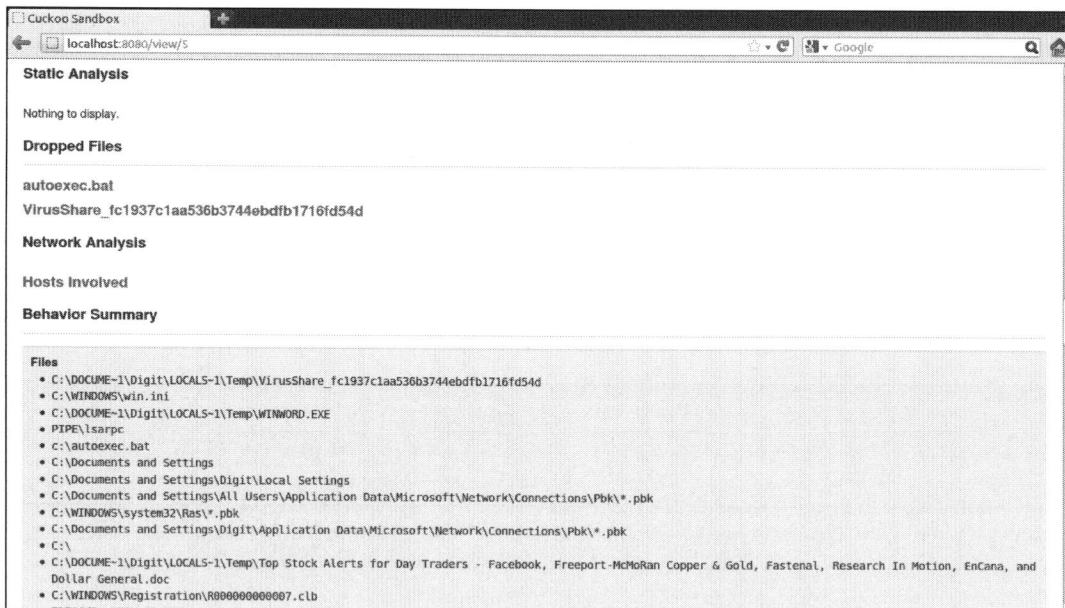

We can see the **Behavior Summary** in the preceding screenshot. When we execute the binary file it will trigger a WordPad application, and open a document: **Top stock alert for Day Trader Facebook**.

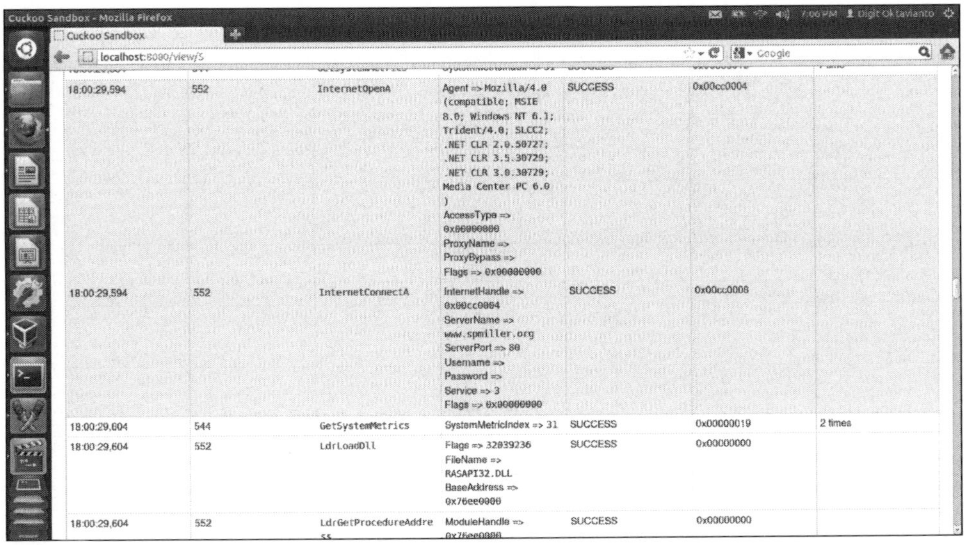

Besides the fact that the malware also dropped `autoexec.bat` in the `c` drive, as you know `autoexec.bat` originally can be found in a DOS-type operating system, most likely it is for executing the malware automatically from inside the infected system. As we can see from `WINWORD.exe` in the following screenshot, there is something interesting:

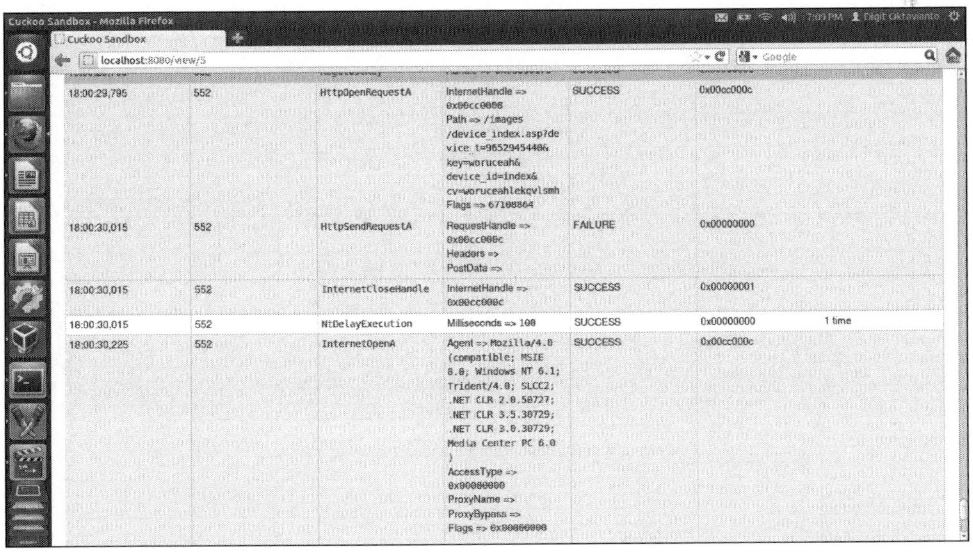

The malicious sample tries to get Internet access, contact a host `www.spmiller.org`, and send an HTTP request to the URL using POST method. Based on Microsoft Windows documentation in `http://msdn.microsoft.com/en-us/library/windows/desktop/aa384233(v=vs.85).aspx`, the `HttpOpenRequest` function creates a new HTTP request handle and stores the specified parameters in that handle. An HTTP request handle holds a request that is to be sent to an HTTP server and contains all `RFC822/MIME/HTTP` headers to be sent as part of the request.

Always learn everything from the analysis results and pay attention to its details. Remember Google is your library. There may be others who have found the same thing as we were doing, so we will crosscheck the results.

Ok, it is about time for us to analyze the memory dump process using Volatility. First of all, we have to check the imageinfo from the memory dump process from Cuckoo Sandbox, which is located at `cuckoo/storage/analysis/(task_id)/memory.dmp`. You can check using this command:

```
$ vol.py -f cuckoo/data/storage/analysis/6/memory.dmp imageinfo
```

```
digit@digit-labs:~$ vol.py -f cuckoo/storage/analyses/6/memory.dmp imageinfo
Volatile Systems Volatility Framework 2.3_beta
Determining profile based on KDBG search...

          Suggested Profile(s) : WinXPSP2x86, WinXPSP3x86 (Instantiated with Win
XPSP2x86)
                     AS Layer1 : IA32PagedMemory (Kernel AS)
                     AS Layer2 : VirtualBoxCoreDumpElf64 (Unnamed AS)
                     AS Layer3 : FileAddressSpace (/home/digit/cuckoo/storage/an
alyses/6/memory.dmp)
                      PAE type : No PAE
                           DTB : 0x39000L
                          KDBG : 0x8054cde0L
          Number of Processors : 1
     Image Type (Service Pack) : 3
                KPCR for CPU 0 : 0xffdff000L
             KUSER_SHARED_DATA : 0xffdf0000L
           Image date and time : 2013-06-09 13:56:45 UTC+0000
     Image local date and time : 2013-06-09 20:56:45 +0700
digit@digit-labs:~$ 
```

As we can see, from the **KDBG** search, the suggestion profile that we can use is **WindowsXPSP2x86** or **WinXPSP3x86**. We will check more details about the memory process. You can use the following command to get more details on the `WinXPSP2x86` profile:

```
$ vol.py psxview --profile=WinXPSP2x86 -f cuckoo/storage/analyses/..
..5/memory.dmp
```

In the preceding screenshot, we can see the details about the process when the malicious file is being executed in our Windows VM. Let's check the suspicious process.

We know that our VM suddenly opens a WordPad application and a file, so let's find the WINWORD process:

```
digit@digit-labs: ~
root@digi... ✖  root@digi... ✖  digit@digi... ✖  digit@digi... ✖  digit@digi... ✖  digit@digi... ✖
     True
0x02a004b0 lsass.exe            672 True    True    True    True    True  True
     True
0x029e8808 svchost.exe          964 True    True    True    True    True  True
     True
0x02969980 spoolsv.exe         1440 True    True    True    True    True  True
     True
0x02836da0 WINWORD.EXE         1884 True    True    True    True    True  True
     True
0x027a3020 alg.exe              372 True    True    True    True    True  True
     True
0x0277ac98 pythonw.exe         1152 True    True    True    True    True  True
     True
0x0279eda0 wscntfy.exe          396 True    True    True    True    True  True
     True
0x02946308 smss.exe             520 True    True    True    True    False False
     False
0x02bc69c8 System                 4 True    True    True    True    False False
     False
0x027ed650 pythonw.exe          284 True    False   True    False   False False
     False
0x0295b6e8 csrss.exe            584 True    True    True    True    False True
     True
digit@digit-labs:~$
```

In the preceding screenshot, we can see the memory dump has a process called **WINWORD.EXE** with PID **1884** (PID may be different in your system). We can check more details about the WINWORD.exe process using the procexedump command.

```
$ vol.py procexedump –profile=WinXPSP2x86 -f cuckoo/storage/..
..analysis/5/memory.dmp -D ./ -p 1884
```

```
digit@digit-labs: ~
root@digi... ✖  root@digi... ✖  digit@digi... ✖  digit@digi... ✖  digit@digi... ✖  digit@digi... ✖
0x0277ac98 pythonw.exe         1152 True    True    True    True    True  True
     True
0x0279eda0 wscntfy.exe          396 True    True    True    True    True  True
     True
0x02946308 smss.exe             520 True    True    True    True    False False
     False
0x02bc69c8 System                 4 True    True    True    True    False False
     False
0x027ed650 pythonw.exe          284 True    True    False   True    False False
     False
0x0295b6e8 csrss.exe            584 True    True    True    True    False True
     True
digit@digit-labs:~$
digit@digit-labs:~$ vol.py procexedump --profile=WinXPSP2x86 -f cuckoo/storage/a
nalyses/5/memory.dmp -D ./ -p 1884
Volatile Systems Volatility Framework 2.3_beta
Process(V) ImageBase Name                 Result
---------- --------- ------------------- ------
0x82836da0 0x00400000 WINWORD.EXE         OK: executable.1884.exe
digit@digit-labs:~$ strings cuckoo/storage/analyses/5/
analysis.log  dump.pcap    logs/       reports/
binary        files/       memory.dmp   shots/
digit@digit-labs:~$ strings executable.1884.exe |egrep '.{6,}' |sort -u| less
digit@digit-labs:~$
```

Okay, let's check the result from the process dump using the strings command:

```
$ strings executable.1884.exe |egrep '.{6,}' |sort -u | less
```

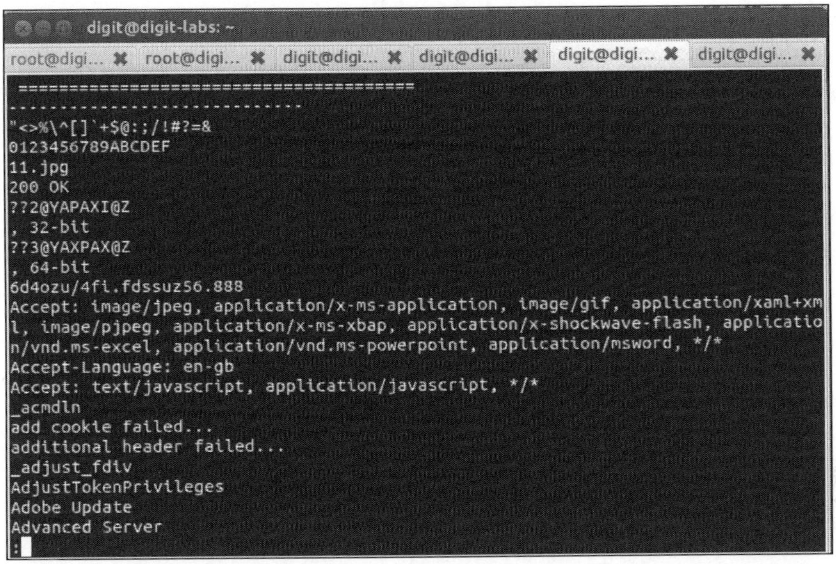

Wow! In the following screenshot, try to take a closer look at the process dump. You will see an interesting value:

E:\XiaoMe\AiH\20120410\Attack\MiniAsp3\Release\MiniAsp.pdb

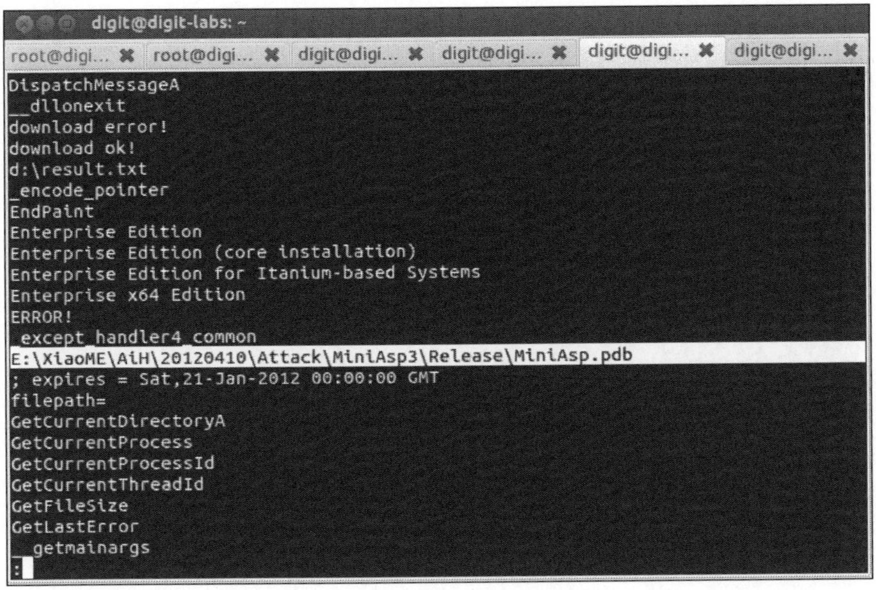

It seems that we have some HTTP request from that file, as we can see in the following screenshot:

```
digit@digit-labs: ~
root@digi... ✖   root@digi... ✖   digit@digi... ✖   digit@digi... ✖   digit@digi... ✖   digit@digi... ✖
;H|sBh
http://
HTTP/1.0
HttpAddRequestHeadersA
HttpEndRequestA
HttpOpenRequestA
HttpQueryInfoA
https://
http://%s/about.htm
http://%s/device_command.asp?device_id=%s&cv=%s&command=%s
http://%s/device_input.asp?device_t=%s&key=%s&device_id=%s&cv=%s
http://%s/device_%s.asp?device_t=%s&key=%s&device_id=%s&cv=%s
HttpSendRequestA
HttpSendRequestExA
http://%s/record.asp?device_t=%s&key=%s&device_id=%s&cv=%s&result=%s
http://%s/result_%s.htm
|                id  :%s
_initterm
_initterm_e
InterlockedCompareExchange
InterlockedExchange
InternetAttemptConnect
InternetCloseHandle
:
```

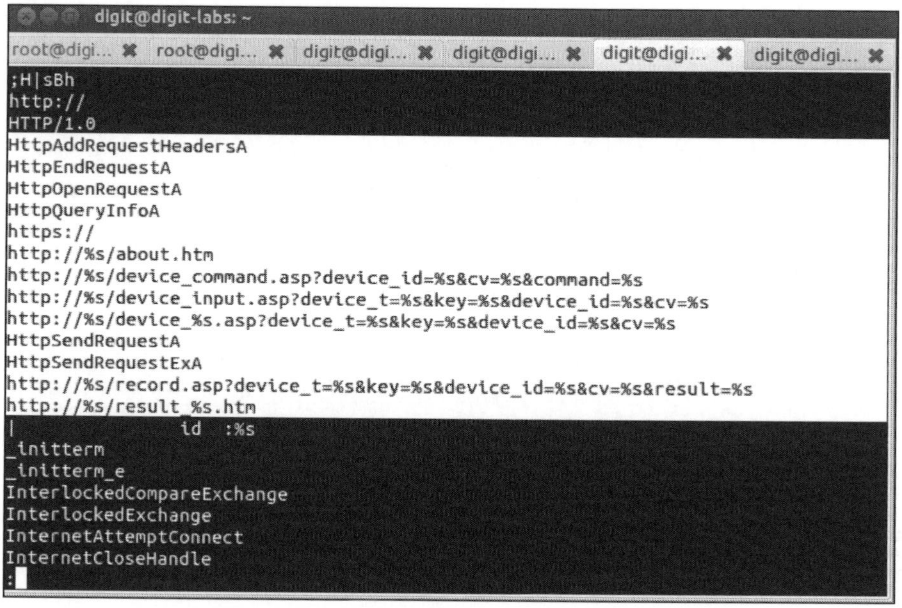

Yes! We have more clues. It is a **MiniASP**, as shown in the following screenshot:

```
digit@digit-labs: ~
root@digi... ✖   root@digi... ✖   digit@digi... ✖   digit@digi... ✖   digit@digi... ✖   digit@digi... ✖
_localtime64
_localtime64_s
LookupAccountSidA
LookupPrivilegeValueA
malloc
_mbschr
memcpy
memset
Microsoft
miniasp
MiniAsp
MINIASP
mode 0
mode 1
|              mode:%s
Mozilla/4.0 (compatible; MSIE 8.0; Windows NT 6.1; Trident/4.0; SLCC2; .NET CLR
2.0.50727; .NET CLR 3.5.30729; .NET CLR 3.0.30729; Media Center PC 6.0 )
MSVCR90.dll
no command
ntdll.dll
NtQuerySystemInformation
_onexit
open internet failed...
:
```

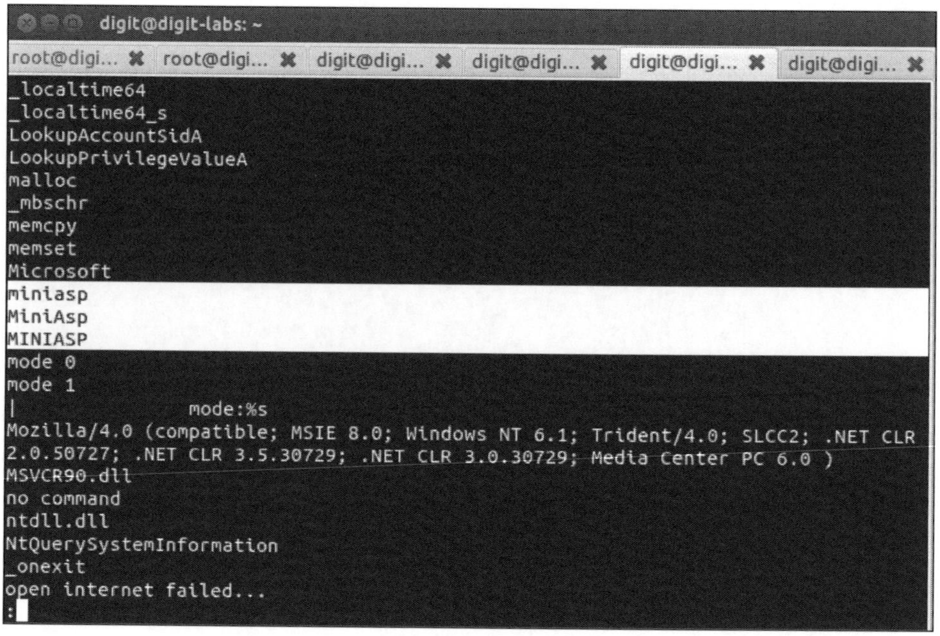

From the suspicious process, we can make a Yara rule that classifies this malware. We will try to make a Yara rule in this section:

1. Create a file called `miniasp3_mem.yar` and you can put it in the `cuckoo/data/yara/` folder.

2. Fill that file with the following rule:

```
rule MiniAsp3_mem {
    meta:
        author = "chort (@chort0)"
        description = "Detect MiniASP3 in memory"
    strings:
        $pdb = "MiniAsp3\\Release\\MiniAsp.pdb" fullword
        $httpAbout = "http://%s/about.htm" fullword
        $httpResult = "http://%s/result_%s.htm" fullword
        $msgInetFail = "open internet failed..." fullword
        $msgRunErr = "run error!" fullword
        $msgRunOk = "run ok!" fullword
        $msgTimeOutM0 = "time out,change to mode 0"
            fullword
        $msgCmdNull = "command is null!" fullword
    condition:
        ($pdb and (all of ($http*)) and any of ($msg*))
}
```

Okay, based on the rule we have just created, we can check the memory dump process (write this command in one line using your terminal):

```
$ vol.py yarascan -profile=WinXPSP2x86 -f cuckoo/storage..
../analysis/5/memory.dmp -y cuckoo/data/yara/miniasp3_mem.yar
```

Ahaa! The rule works well. Let's try to scan our home directory to check the files that go into our Yara rule classification:

```
$ yara -r cuckoo/data/yara/miniasp3_mem.yar /home/digit
```

Wow, now we can see that there are some files that are associated with the **MiniASP** malware based on our Yara rule. Interesting, isn't it? We have found so much in the memory and Volatility can do a great job.

Summary

After analyzing an APT1 malware sample, we can discover some typical activities performed by the malware. We learned how to create a rule based on the Yara signature to detect the presence of APT1 malware. Of course, this cannot be done without the help of Volatility in memory forensics. A strong knowledge in memory forensic is needed while performing analysis in APT1 malware sample is needed, because they can easily fool us with unexpected conditions. That is when experience comes in handy; so keep learning from new and old malware and always share your findings on the Internet so that others can learn from it, especially right now during the time of the rise of document-based malware, and when we are on the losing side in the war against malware.

We also learned that some malware can detect the presence of debuggers or virtualization environments; however, we will learn to handle these kinds of obstacles in *Chapter 5, Tips and Tricks for Cuckoo Sandbox*. But before that, in the next chapter, we will learn about the most important stage in malware analysis. It will involve learning how to make a report malware analysis using Cuckoo Sandbox reporting tools, or exporting the output data report to another format for advanced report analysis.

4
Reporting with Cuckoo Sandbox

In previous chapters, you may have seen the reports after all the processing done by Cuckoo. By default, Cuckoo has several reporting formats, such as human-readable format, **MAEC (Malware Attribute Enumeration and Characterization)** format—a standard language developed by MITRE—and the ability to export a data report to another format. This chapter will describe more about reporting modules in Cuckoo, such as how to:

- Create a built-in report in HTML format
- Create a MAEC report
- Export data report analysis from Cuckoo to another format

By the end of this chapter, we will learn how to make a malware analysis report using Cuckoo Sandbox reporting tools. We will also learn how to export the output data report to another format for advanced report analysis.

Creating a built-in report in HTML format

Basically, Cuckoo will make an HTML report by using the template that you may have found in Cuckoo's subdirectory `data/html`. The main HTML template file is `report.html` with the addition of a few other HTML and CSS files, as shown in the following screenshot:

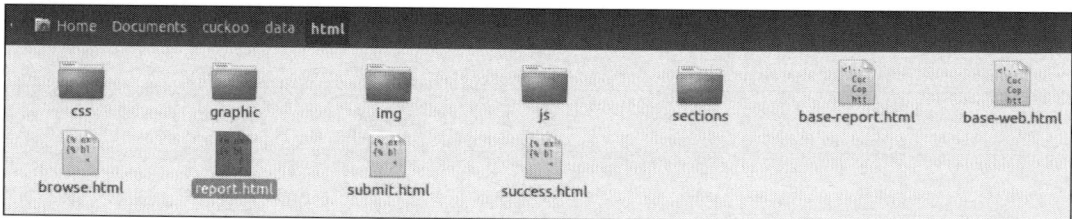

If you find some malware and analyze it as explained earlier in *Chapter 2, Using Cuckoo Sandbox to Analyze a Sample Malware*, you already know that the result will occur like the following screenshot:

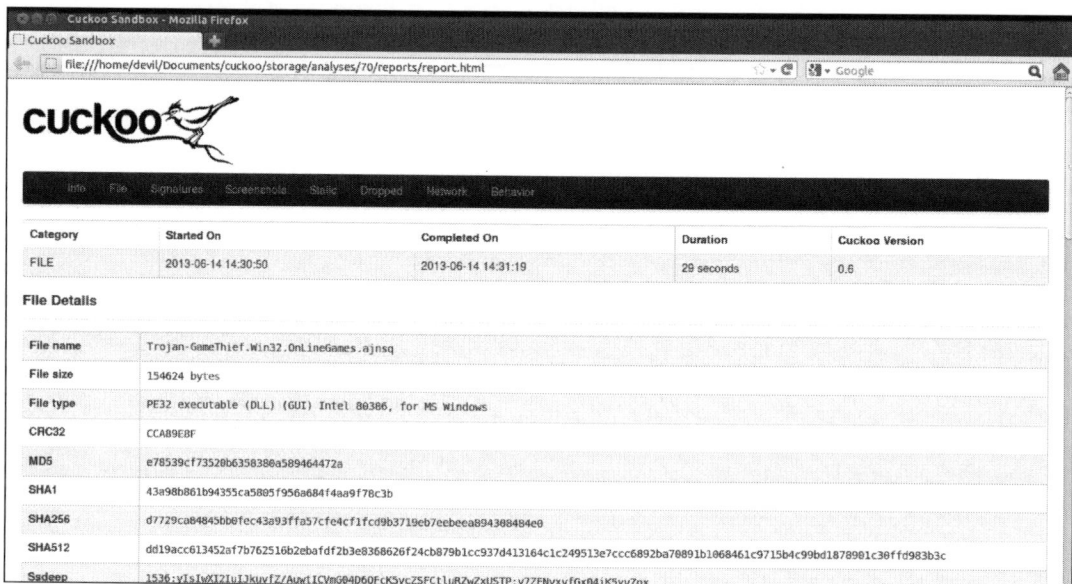

There are a few tabs available in the HTML reports. They are **Info**, **File**, **Signatures**, **Screenshots**, **Static**, **Dropped**, **Network**, and **Behavior**. The information included in each tab is generated based on the malware, what happens when analyzing the malware, and so on. Not all of the sections need to be generated by Cuckoo. Things that didn't occur or failed to be generated may not be available in Cuckoo Sandbox HTML Report.

Cuckoo Sandbox HTML Reports	
Info	This tab shows the category of the analyzed malware and consists of the following nested tabs:
	Category (File or URL), **Started On**, **Completed On**, **Duration**, and **Cuckoo Version**
File	The information under this tab is contained under the **File Details** tab. It shows all of the analyzed malware file details, consisting of:
	File name, **File size**, **File type**, **CRC32**, **MD5**, **SHA1**, **SHA256**, **SHA512**, **Ssdeep**, **PEiD**, **Yara**, and **VirusTotal**
Signatures	The signature of the malware based on severity of matches
Screenshot	The screenshots of what happened in the Guest OS after executing the malware
Static Analysis	This shows details about static analysis and consists of the following sections:
	Version Infos, **Sections**, **Resources**, **Imports**, and **Exports**
Dropped Files	The dropped filenames that may be created by the malware
Network	This tab shows the details of the network activities and consists of the following sections:
	Hosts Involved, **DNS Requests**, **HTTP Requests**, and **IRC Requests**
Behavior	This tab shows details of what the malware did in the system and consists of the following sections:
	Files, **Mutexes**, **Registry Keys**, and **Processes**

The module script that will be used by Cuckoo to generate the HTML report is available at the subfolder of Cuckoo—`modules/reporting/reporthtml.py`. We will use this module later and edit the module to make another type of output report.

Creating a MAEC Report

According to the official website of **MAEC (Malware Attribute Enumeration and Characterization)** — http://maec.mitre.org/:

> *"MAEC is a standardized language for encoding and communicating high-fidelity information about malware based upon attributes such as behaviors, artifacts, and attack patterns."*

It eliminates the ambiguity and inaccuracy of malware descriptions and reduces the reliance on signatures, which helps MAEC to:

- Improve human-to-human, human-to-tool, tool-to-tool, and tool-to-human communication about malware

- Reduce potential duplication of malware analysis efforts by researchers

- Allow for the faster development of countermeasures by enabling the ability to leverage responses to previously observed malware instances

This is shown in the following screenshot:

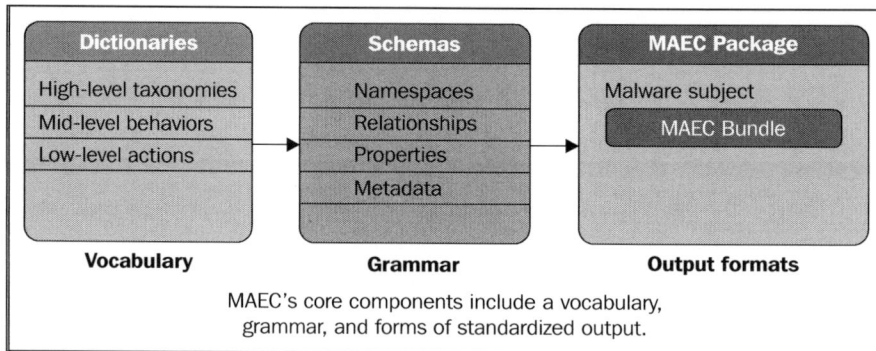

Dictionaries	Schemas	MAEC Package
High-level taxonomies	Namespaces	Malware subject
Mid-level behaviors	Relationships	MAEC Bundle
Low-level actions	Properties	
	Metadata	
Vocabulary	**Grammar**	**Output formats**

MAEC's core components include a vocabulary, grammar, and forms of standardized output.

The malware reporting lacked a common structure and vocabulary; it often excluded key malware attributes that may be useful for mitigation and detection purposes, such as the specific vulnerability being exploited. So, it needs to be made in a common format and made a standard in malware reporting analysis.

The use of MAEC's standardized vocabulary and grammar in malware reporting will facilitate the creation of a separate and uniform reporting format. Such a format will reduce confusion as to the nature of malware threats through the accurate and unambiguous communication of malware attributes, while also ensuring uniformity between reports composed by disparate authors and organizations — as mentioned at https://maec.mitre.org/language/usecases.html.

In Cuckoo Sandbox, there is a module called [maec11] in the reporting.conf file. Make sure it's **enabled** value is **on**. Start your cuckoo.py, or if you have started it, turn it off by *Ctrl + C* and start it again to make sure the settings take changes, as shown in the following screenshot:

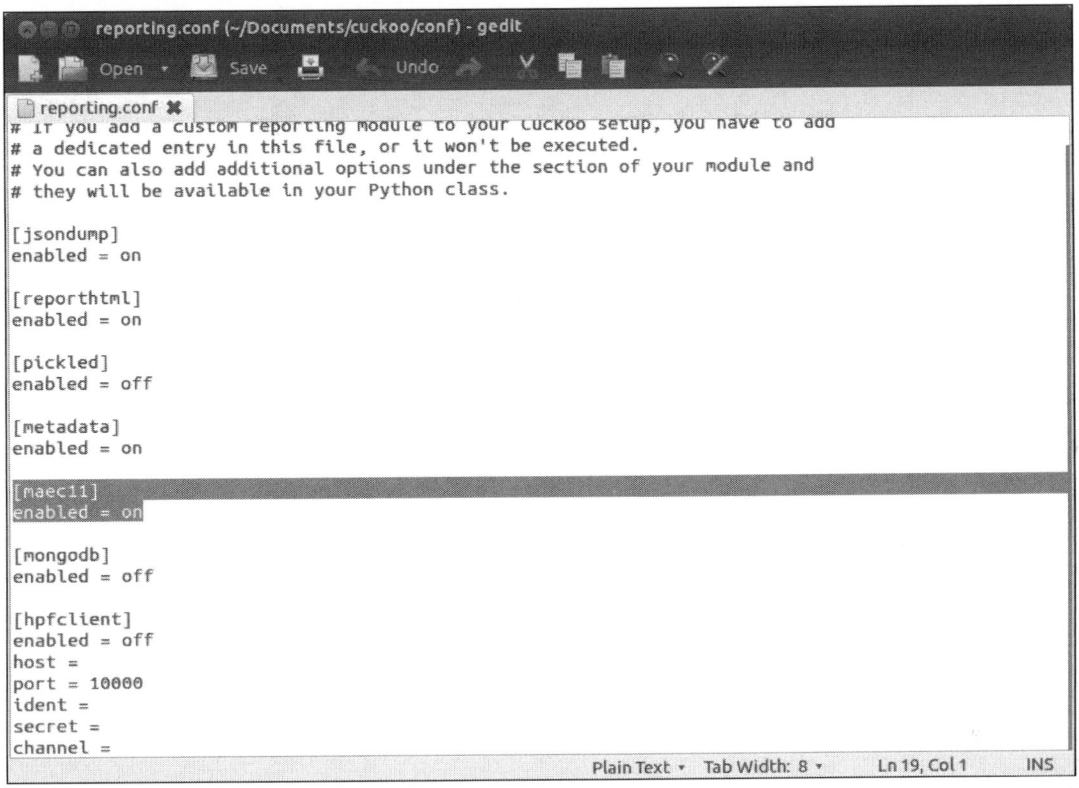

Let's start a submitting process. Just as I've explained in *Chapter 2, Using Cuckoo Sandbox to Analyze a Sample Malware*, we'll start the submitting process by typing this command:

```
$ python utils/submit.py --package exe  shares/Conficker.C.exe
```

Our virtual machine will now open the malware. There might be no action taken on your Windows OS, but the background process is still running. This is because the Conficker C.exe file is just a network malware. After the analysis time is up (not because the malware stopped running), the virtual machine will be turned off automatically.

We can find the result in the **reports** subfolder located at `storage/analyses/<your task ID>/reports`.

Let's look at the preceding screenshot. The `reports` subfolder contains the report files in several formats such as HTML, JSON, XML, and PDF, and we will discuss this later in this chapter. In the previous chapter, usually we would open the `report.html` file, but because we're talking about reporting malware analysis in MAEC format, we will now open the `report.maec-1.1.xml` file. If you double-click it, it may open in your web browser, as shown in the following screenshot:

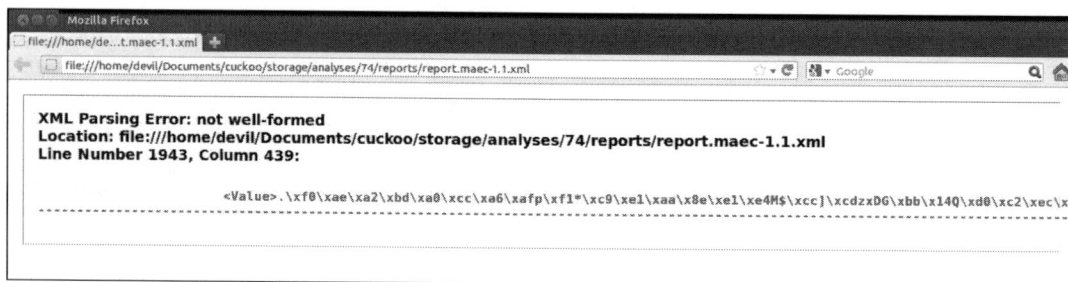

Unfortunately, this time the browser didn't recognize the MAEC report. As shown in the preceding screenshot, we encountered an **XML Parsing Error: not well-formed** error especially in **Line Number 1943, Column 439**.

Let's see what we have got in report.maec-1.1.xml. You can open `report.maec-1.1.xml` in **gedit** or any of your favorite text editors:

Well, as it turns out, it is in the raw format of XML. A bit confusing, isn't it? We need a little help from another tool to read the report. There's a bunch of XML editors in the wild with a "must purchase" license or a free license, for example, **Oxygen XML Editor**, **EditiX XML Editor**, **XML Copy Editor**, **TreeLine**, and many more. You may already have a specific tool for viewing and editing XML so please don't hesitate to use it. But if you do not, you may use TreeLine as it is a free XML editor and it is a powerful and easy-to-use tool for a beginner.

There are two easy ways to install TreeLine, by using the Ubuntu Software Center or using the `apt-get` command line. If you want to use the Ubuntu Software Center to install TreeLine, you need to:

1. Open your Ubuntu Software Center.
2. Search for `treeline` in the search textbox in the top-right corner of the window.

3. Click on **Install**, put your Ubuntu password in the dialog box, and hit **Authenticate**. Wait for the download and installation process to complete.

After the installation is completed, you will see TreeLine in the left dock bar.

If you want to use the `apt-get` command line to install TreeLine, carry out the following steps:

1. Open the terminal and run the following command:

```
$ sudo apt-get install treeline
```

2. Type in your password and continue the installation.

Now, let's try to use TreeLine to open the MAEC report. From the dock bar, open TreeLine. Then open the MAEC report that was previously generated from Cuckoo's malware analysis. In this case, we will open the MAEC report from the previous task ID (ID number 60). Now, open the document and choose **Generic XML (Non-TreeLine File)** and click on **OK**.

We will see the document in TreeLine appear, as shown in the following screenshot:

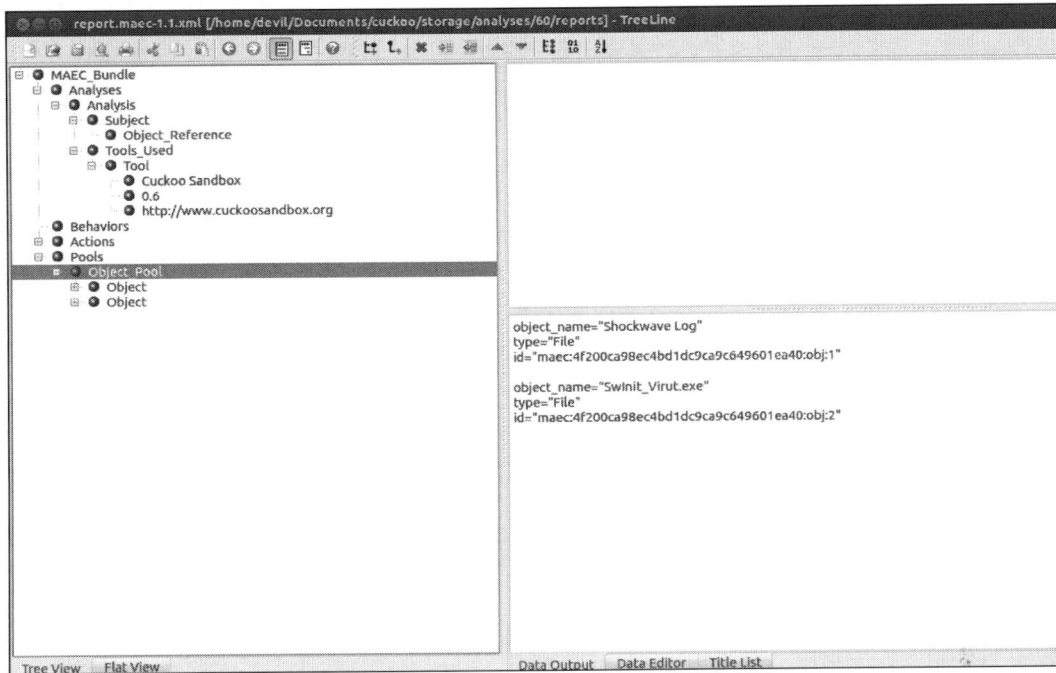

And that's the report in MAEC format, which can be used for cross-platform software, such as Cuckoo. Remember to share your findings with the malware and security community, such as `contagiodump.blogspot.in` and `malwaremustdie.blogspot.in`.

Exporting data report analysis from Cuckoo to another format

We may see some type of report that Cuckoo generated. Basically, there are seven reporting modules available to users and all of them depend on user preferences. If you want a report that will work as a cross-platform software with another malware analyzer, you might want to use the MAEC platform. If you want to use a report that may be used in another software that is using JSON as input format, you might want to use the JSON platform. Options are there for you to choose depending upon your needs. But, occasionally, people might want to use another format too.

So, is it possible to make another report format rather than the regular one Cuckoo supplied? Well, actually it's possible. We all know that Cuckoo is an open source software that uses Python programming language. The codes are available and it's editable. So, in this section, we will modify the `report.html` module to create a new report file format. It will make a report in PDF format called `report.pdf` after successfully generating the `report.html` module.

We can use the tool named **wkhtmltopdf**. Although there are other good or even better tools that we can use, but some of them require paid licenses. Another useful tool we can use is **Python-PDFKit** which is available at `https://github.com/JazzCore/python-pdfkit`.

So, what is `wkhtmltopdf`? It is a command-line program that permits to create a PDF from a URL, a local HTML file or stdin. It will make a PDF file with the Webkit Engine. This program requires an X11 server to run. Python-PDFKit is a Python 2 and 3 wrapper for the `wkhtmltopdf` utility to convert HTML to PDF using Webkit. It's just like an API for supporting `wkhtmltopdf` so that this command-line tool can be used in our Python programs with some options available. The first thing we'll do is install `wkhtmltopdf`:

1. Start the installation of `wkhtmltopdf` using the following command:

    ```
    $ sudo apt-get install wkhtmltopdf
    ```

2. After the installation process is finished, we have to download the Python-PDFKit tool. We can find it at `https://github.com/JazzCore/python-pdfkit/archive/master.zip`.

    As usual for the GitHub files, we will use git clone:

    ```
    $ git clone https://github.com/JazzCore/python-pdfkit.git
    ```

3. When we're done cloning it, we will navigate to the directory python-pdfkit under the Documents folder:

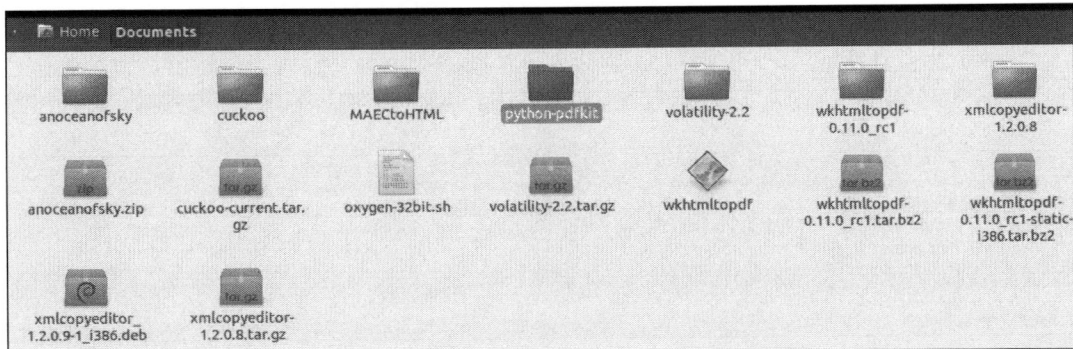

Inside the python-pdfkit folder, there is a file named setup.py. This is the installation setup for Python-PDFKit. We'll use this so that the library can be used in our coding later.

4. Change the directory to python-pdfkit and simply run this command:

```
$ sudo python setup.py build
```

5. Then install it using this command:

```
$ sudo python setup.py install
```

Now the installation of this tool is finished. Let's try to modify the code in reporthtml.py. We can find reporthtml.py in the subfolder modules/reporting/. First, we need to delete reporthtml.pyc to make sure that Cuckoo will compile our new modified code and make it new again:

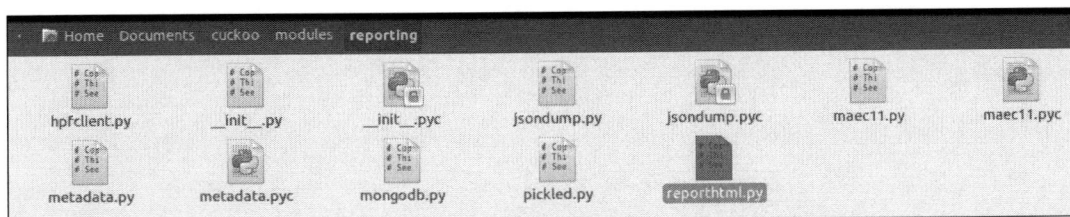

But before we continue our progress to modify the report.html module, we must first understand how the code in the Cuckoo module works.

Cuckoo starts processing malware analyses in raw results, and then the results are abstracted by the processing modules and then the global container is generated. After that, it will be passed to the reporting module that is available in the configuration file (conf/reporting.conf).

As an example to understand the workflow, we will understand how the JSON dump reporting module works. As you may have seen in the `conf/reporting.conf` file, there is a module that is written as shown the following screenshot:

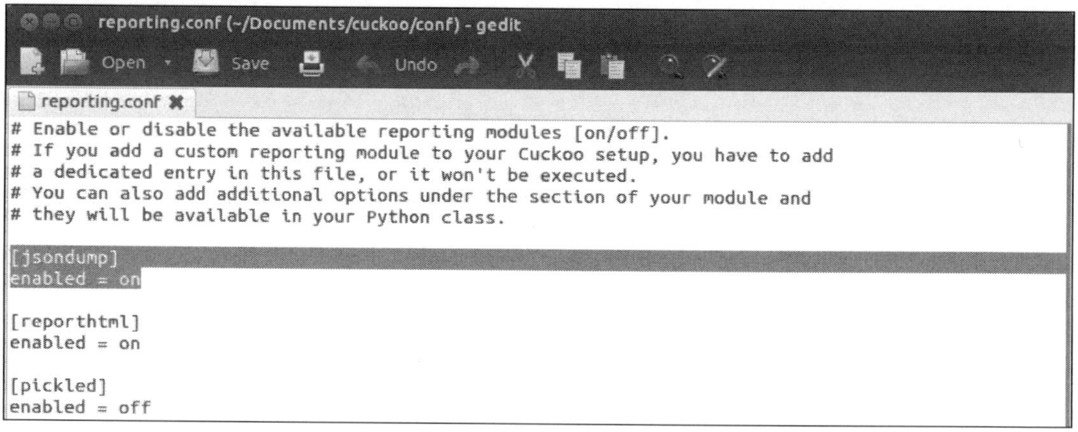

Actually, the module name in `reporting.conf` is a filename for the Python-coded file in the folder `/modules/reporting`. We can see it as a file named `jsondump.py`. The code in `jsondump.py` is shown in the following screenshot:

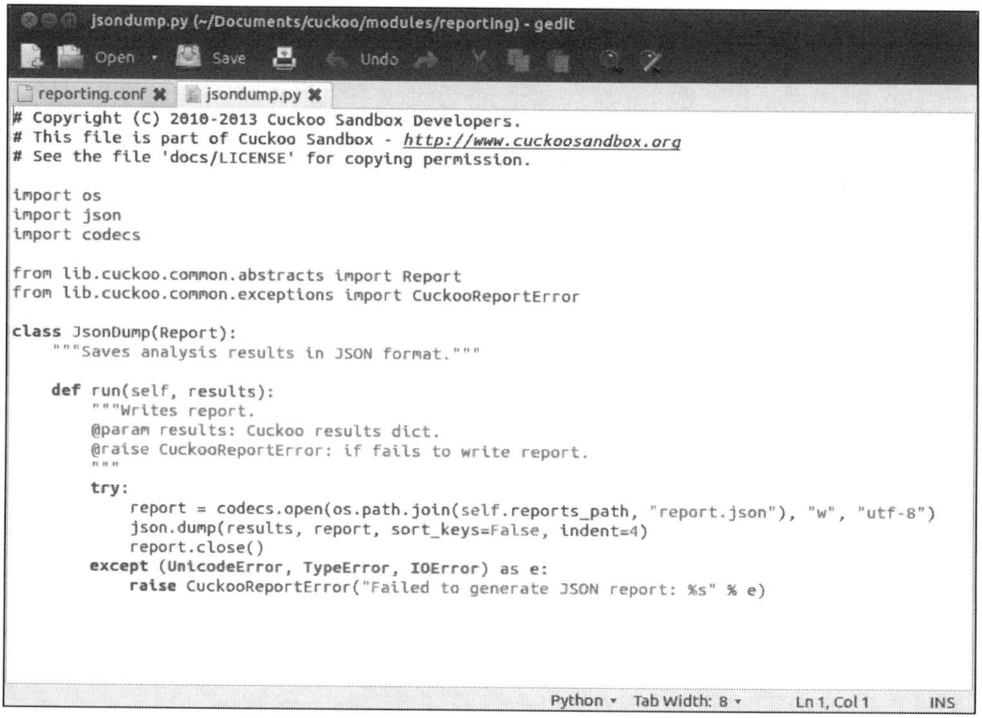

This is a simple code that basically receives the global container produced by the processing modules, converts it into JSON, and writes it to a file in JSON format. All the code in the reporting module must pass the following requirements:

- The class must import the Report class
- Have a run() function performing the main operations
- Try to catch most exceptions and raise a CuckooReportError error to notify the issue

The code also may have some attributes that are available in Cuckoo:

- self.analysis_path: This attribute stores the path to the folder containing the raw analysis results (for example, storage/analyses/1/)
- self.reports_path: This attribute stores the path to the folder where the reports should be written (for example, storage/analyses/1/reports/)
- self.conf_path: This attribute stores the path to the analysis.conf file of the current analysis (for example storage/analyses/1/analysis.conf)
- self.options: This attribute stores a dictionary containing all the options specified in the report.html module's configuration section in conf/reporting.conf

Have you understood how the Cuckoo report module works now? Great, now let's create and modify the code.

1. Make a new file called pdfs.py.

    We will not list the module in the reporting.conf file because we want to create a PDF report exactly after the HTML report has been created.

2. Open pdfs.py in your text editor, in this case we will use gedit.

3. Type in the code as shown in the following screenshot:

```
import pdfkit

def create_pdf(xhtml, dest):
    pdfkit.from_file(xhtml, dest)
```

4. Always remember to save it.

5. Then open the `reporthtml.py` file and add the `import` statement just as it is highlighted in the following screenshot:

6. Then add some additional code after the words `try` and `except`, as shown in the following screenshot, to generate `report.html`:

> We need to pay attention to the indentation of the preceding code as it is Python programming language. Python pays attention to the indentations used in the code.

Now, we will restart Cuckoo Sandbox to find out whether the code we developed earlier is working properly or not. If the code was written properly, then Cuckoo Sandbox will run without any error.

Try to submit a malware for testing the module. If the analysis process was successfully done, then the result will be shown as in the following screenshot:

As we can see, Cuckoo Sandbox analysis is working properly. The reports generation has been completed and saved with a task ID. Let's see the result in the directory based on your task ID:

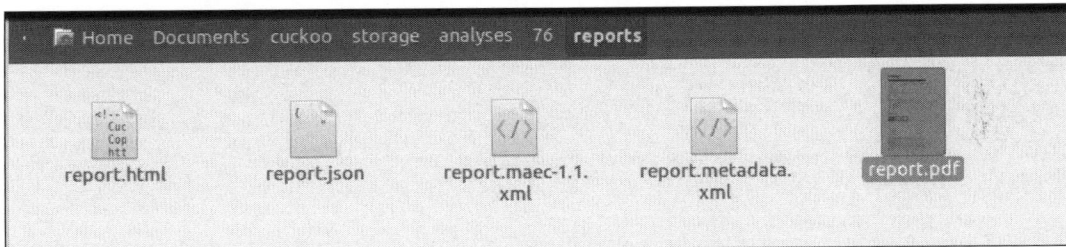

We will see the generated file—`report.pdf`—in the `reports` directory. You can open it using your default PDF viewer:

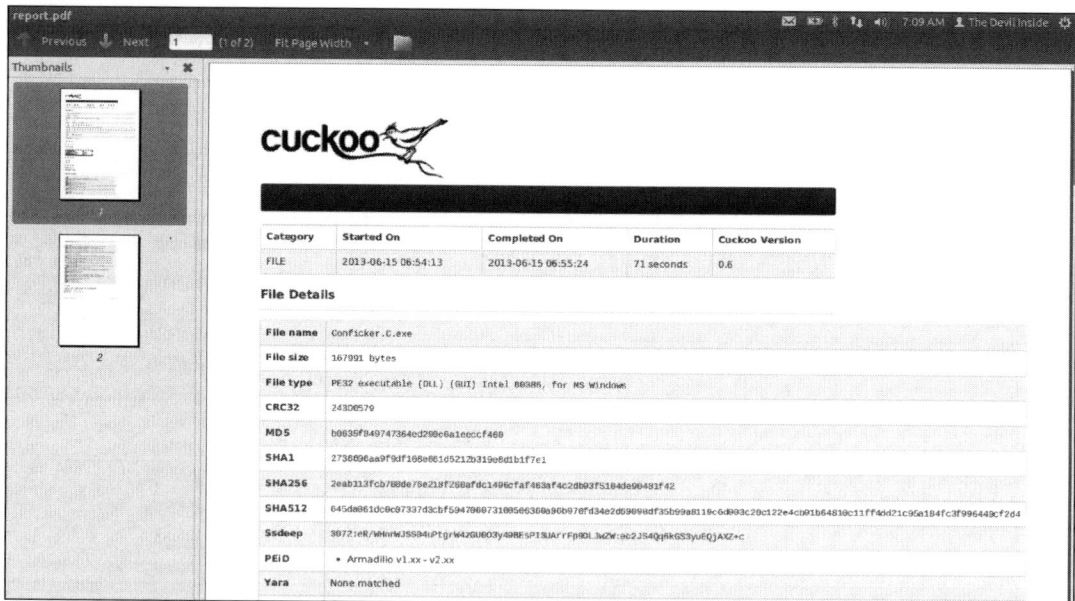

That's it! Now we have the `report` file in the most used document format in the world.

Summary

In this chapter, we learned the ways of reporting a malware analysis in the form of different formats other than Cuckoo's standard HTML reports. We learned how to export the reports in another format by modifying some of the configuration files and also learned about the MAEC standard. It's important to have a report that everyone can share in the same language so that it can be used for further analysis.

In the next chapter, we will learn several tips and tricks for enhancing Cuckoo's ability in the malware analysis process. Some people from the community created interesting plugins or modules which will help users perform new experiments using Cuckoo Sandbox. Can't wait, can you? Me neither.

5
Tips and Tricks for Cuckoo Sandbox

In the final chapter of this book, we will be covering some tips and tricks for Cuckoo Sandbox. We need to modify Cuckoo so that it becomes harder to be detected as a Sandbox by malware, or further enhance the malware analysis process by adding plugins or modules. By doing so, we expect that Cuckoo is able to monitor the malware inch by inch so that we can capture the malware, just like in live infected hosts, and with more plugins or modules, Cuckoo will be able to run malware in many environments or make malware analysis easier, faster, and more of a pleasure than a routine task over and over again.

In this chapter, there will be three topics. They are:

- Hardening Cuckoo Sandbox against VM detection
- Cuckooforcanari – integrating Cuckoo Sandbox with the Maltego project
- Automating e-mail attachments with Cuckoo MX

Hardening Cuckoo Sandbox against VM detection

In recent cases, some malware are checking the environment when being executed. These malware will not run in virtualization products, such as VirtualBox, VMware, KVM. Alberto Ortega wrote of an interesting way of hardening Cuckoo Sandbox against malware that can detect the presence of virtualizations.

As written in `labs.alienvault.com`, we will use **Pafish (Paranoid Fish)** to detect if our virtualization environment is able to evade those anti-debuggers/sandboxes/ VMs. Pafish is a tool that can run an anti-debugger/VM/sandbox when executed. These technique are often used by malware to avoid analyses. You can download Pafish at `https://github.com/a0rtega/pafish.git`. For your VM, run the following command lines to install Pafish:

```
$ sudo mkdir pafish
$ sudo git clone https://github.com/a0rtega/pafish.git pafish/
```

One of the core elements of Cuckoo Sandbox is **CuckooMon**, which provides Cuckoo Sandbox with the ability to intercept the execution flow of a potentially malicious malware sample.

Now, let's try to run Pafish in the virtualization OS that we used to run Cuckoo Sandbox:

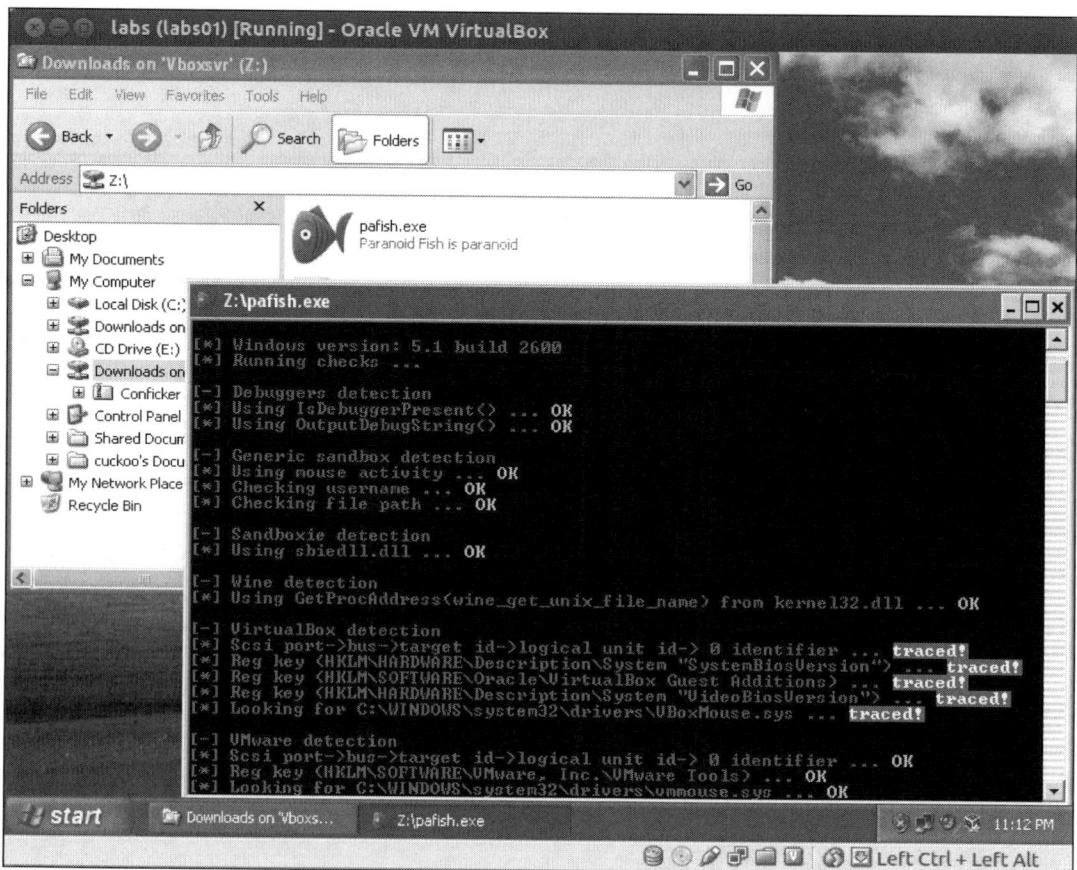

It turns out that Pafish detects debuggers, generic sandboxes, sanboxies using `sbiedll.dll`, Wine emulator by using `GetProcAddress` from `kernel32.dll`, VMware, QEMU, and also VirtualBox that we are already using.

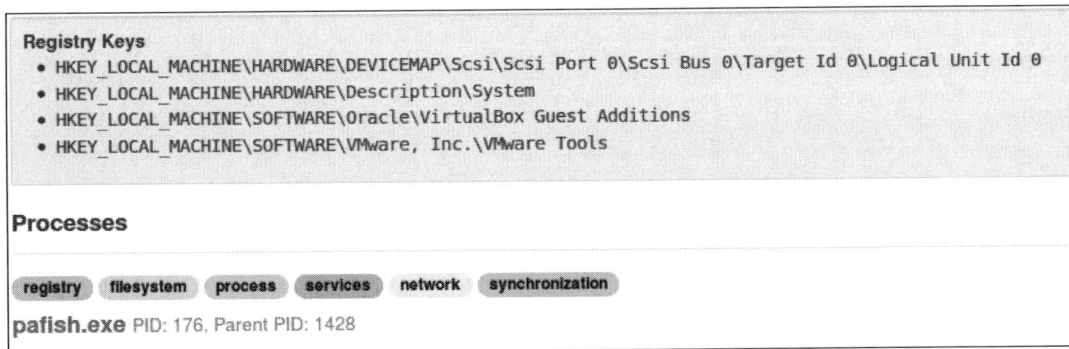

Registry Keys
- HKEY_LOCAL_MACHINE\HARDWARE\DEVICEMAP\Scsi\Scsi Port 0\Scsi Bus 0\Target Id 0\Logical Unit Id 0
- HKEY_LOCAL_MACHINE\HARDWARE\Description\System
- HKEY_LOCAL_MACHINE\SOFTWARE\Oracle\VirtualBox Guest Additions
- HKEY_LOCAL_MACHINE\SOFTWARE\VMware, Inc.\VMware Tools

Processes

registry | filesystem | process | services | network | synchronization

pafish.exe PID: 176, Parent PID: 1428

As we can see in the screenshot with the command prompt window, Pafish sensors detected the VirtualBox environment by looking at:

- **Scsi port**
- Registry key **"SystemBiosVersion"**
- Registry key **VirtualBox Guest Additions**
- Registry key **"VideoBiosVersion"**
- Drivers file **VBoxMouse.sys**

So what we need to do next is figure out how to modify VirtualBox so that the sensors will not be able to read it. The code that handles those hooks is in the `hook_reg.c` file as part of CuckooMon.

Let's download the CuckooMon source code from `https://github.com/cuckoobox/cuckoomon`:

```
$ sudo mkdir cuckoomon
$ sudo git clone https://github.com/cuckoobox/cuckoomoncuckoomon/
```

The downloaded file should contain files as shown in the following screenshot:

```
cuckoo@Ubuntu:~/cuckoomon$ ls
cuckoomon.c          hook_process.c     hook_socket.c    LICENSE.txt   pipe.c
distorm3.2-package   hook_reg.c         hook_special.c   log.c         pipe.h
hook_file.c          hook_reg_native.c  hook_sync.c      log.h         README.md
hooking.c            hook_services.c    hook_thread.c    Makefile      tests
hooking.h            hooks.h            hook_window.c    misc.c        utf8.c
hook_misc.c          hook_sleep.c       ignore.c         misc.h        utf8.h
hook_network.c       hook_sleep.h       ignore.h         ntapi.h
cuckoo@Ubuntu:~/cuckoomon$
```

Now open `hook.reg.c` files and look for the `RegOpenKeyExA` hook. The key here is on `lpSubKey`, it is the one that will check VirtualBox or ControlSet:

```
HOOKDEF(LONG, WINAPI, RegOpenKeyExA,
    __in        HKEY hKey,
    __in_opt    LPCTSTR lpSubKey,
    __reserved  DWORD ulOptions,
    __in        REGSAM samDesired,
    __out       PHKEY phkResult
) {
    LONG ret = Old_RegOpenKeyExA(hKey, lpSubKey, ulOptions, samDesired,
        phkResult);
    LOQ("psP", "Registry", hKey, "SubKey", lpSubKey, "Handle", phkResult);
    return ret;
}
```

So now we can change `LONG ret` into something more defined, such as:

- `lpSubKey` detection for VirtualBox, ControlSet will be set to `!=NULL`
- Otherwise, `ret` will be `= Old_RegOpenKeyExA(hKey, lpSubKey, ulOptions, samDesired, phkResult);`

Whenever the malware tries to find a string like `VirtualBox` or `ControlSet`, the code will log the warning and fake the response and make the malware feel safe to run. The code will look like the following screenshot:

```
/* Hardened */
HOOKDEF(LONG, WINAPI, RegOpenKeyExA,
  __in       HKEY hKey,
  __in_opt   LPCTSTR lpSubKey,
  __reserved DWORD ulOptions,
  __in       REGSAM samDesired,
  __out      PHKEY phkResult
) {
    LONG ret;
    if (strstr(lpSubKey, "VirtualBox") != NULL) {
        ret = 1;
        LOQ("s", "Hardening", "Faked RegOpenKeyExA return");
    }
    else if (strstr(lpSubKey, "ControlSet") != NULL) {
        ret = 1;
        LOQ("s", "Hardening", "Faked RegOpenKeyExA return");
    }
    else {
        ret = Old_RegOpenKeyExA(hKey, lpSubKey, ulOptions, samDesired,
            phkResult);
    }
    LOQ("psP", "Registry", hKey, "SubKey", lpSubKey, "Handle", phkResult);
    return ret;
}
```

And then we need to do the same with `RegQueryValueExA`. See the next screenshot for a better understanding:

```
HOOKDEF(LONG, WINAPI, RegQueryValueExA,
  __in       HKEY hKey,
  __in_opt   LPCTSTR lpValueName,
  __reserved LPDWORD lpReserved,
  __out_opt  LPDWORD lpType,
  __out_opt  LPBYTE lpData,
  __inout_opt LPDWORD lpcbData
) {
    ENSURE_DWORD(lpType);
    LONG ret = Old_RegQueryValueExA(hKey, lpValueName, lpReserved, lpType,
        lpData, lpcbData);
    if(ret == ERROR_SUCCESS && lpType != NULL && lpData != NULL &&
            lpcbData != NULL) {
        LOQ("psr", "Handle", hKey, "ValueName", lpValueName,
            "Data", *lpType, *lpcbData, lpData);
    }
    else {
        LOQ("psLL", "Handle", hKey, "ValueName", lpValueName,
            "Type", lpType, "DataLength", lpcbData);
    }
    return ret;
}
```

The one that we can change is the `lpValueName`. This will search for strings such as `SystemBiosVersion`, `Identifier`, and `ProductId`.

We'll change the response of `lpValueName` for `SystemBiosVersion`, `Identifier` and `ProductId` to `!=NULL`. See this screenshot for a better understanding:

```c
/* Hardened */
HOOKDEF(LONG, WINAPI, RegQueryValueExA,
    __in         HKEY hKey,
    __in_opt     LPCTSTR lpValueName,
    __reserved   LPDWORD lpReserved,
    __out_opt    LPDWORD lpType,
    __out_opt    LPBYTE lpData,
    __inout_opt  LPDWORD lpcbData
) {
    LONG ret;
    if (strstr(lpValueName, "SystemBiosVersion") != NULL) {
        ret = ERROR_SUCCESS;
        LOQ("s", "Hardening", "Faked RegQueryValueExA return");
    }
    else if (strstr(lpValueName, "Identifier") != NULL) {
        ret = ERROR_SUCCESS;
        LOQ("s", "Hardening", "Faked RegQueryValueExA return");
    }
    else if (strstr(lpValueName, "ProductId") != NULL) {
        ret = ERROR_SUCCESS;
        LOQ("s", "Hardening", "Faked RegQueryValueExA return");
    }
    else {
        ret = Old_RegQueryValueExA(hKey, lpValueName, lpReserved, lpType,
            lpData, lpcbData);
    }
    LOQ("psLB", "Handle", hKey, "ValueName", lpValueName,
        "Type", lpType, "Buffer", lpcbData, lpData);
    return ret;
}
```

After we change the files above, if the malware tries to read the registry key it will fail and the malware should be running unless the malware creator set it to be different.

Now, we have to change the call that is used to access the files. The call we used is `GetFileAttributesA` in a file named `hook_file.c`. However, I could not find `GetFileAttributesA` in Cuckoo Version 0.6, even when I tried to find it in the terminal:

```
$ grep -r getfile*.c
```

Nevertheless, we will try to compile the `cuckoomon.dll` source code with the file we changed before (`hook.reg.c`).

1. Let's install **mingw**:

   ```
   $ sudo apt-get install mingw32
   ```

2. Open `Makefile` in the source code and run the following command lines:

   ```
   $ sudo vim Makefile
   ```

3. Change `CC = gcc` with `CC = /usr/bin/i586-mingw32msvc-gcc`

4. Now compile the DLL file:

   ```
   $ sudo make
   ```

5. Copy the resulting file (`cuckoomon.dll`) into the `cuckoo/analyzer/windows/dll/` folder.

   We can replace it while Cuckoo Sandbox is running.

6. Next, we'll try to submit `pafish.exe` again to Cuckoo Sandbox:

```
C:\DOCUME~1\ikons\LOCALS~1\Temp\pafish.exe                          - □ ×

[-] Sandboxie detection
[*] Using sbiedll.dll ... OK

[-] Wine detection
[*] Using GetProcAddress(wine_get_unix_file_name) from kernel32.dll ... OK

[-] VirtualBox detection
[*] Scsi port->bus->target id->logical unit id-> 0 identifier ... OK
[*] Reg key (HKLM\HARDWARE\Description\System "SystemBiosVersion") ... OK
[*] Reg key (HKLM\SOFTWARE\Oracle\VirtualBox Guest Additions) ... OK
[*] Reg key (HKLM\HARDWARE\Description\System "VideoBiosVersion") ... traced!
[*] Looking for C:\WINDOWS\system32\drivers\VBoxMouse.sys ... traced!

[-] VMware detection
[*] Scsi port->bus->target id->logical unit id-> 0 identifier ... OK
[*] Reg key (HKLM\SOFTWARE\VMware, Inc.\VMware Tools) ... OK
[*] Looking for C:\WINDOWS\system32\drivers\vmmouse.sys ... OK
[*] Looking for C:\WINDOWS\system32\drivers\vmhgfs.sys ... OK

[-] Qemu detection
[*] Scsi port->bus->target id->logical unit id-> 0 identifier ... OK
[*] Reg key (HKLM\HARDWARE\Description\System "SystemBiosVersion") ... OK

[-] Finished, feel free to RE me.
```

Now, there are only two registries that remain being traced. One thing I did try is running cuckoomon.dll from the link given in labs.alienvault.com and its not working. We compare the downloaded DLL file with the file we compiled ourselves. This will cause Pafish to crash, as shown in the following screenshot:

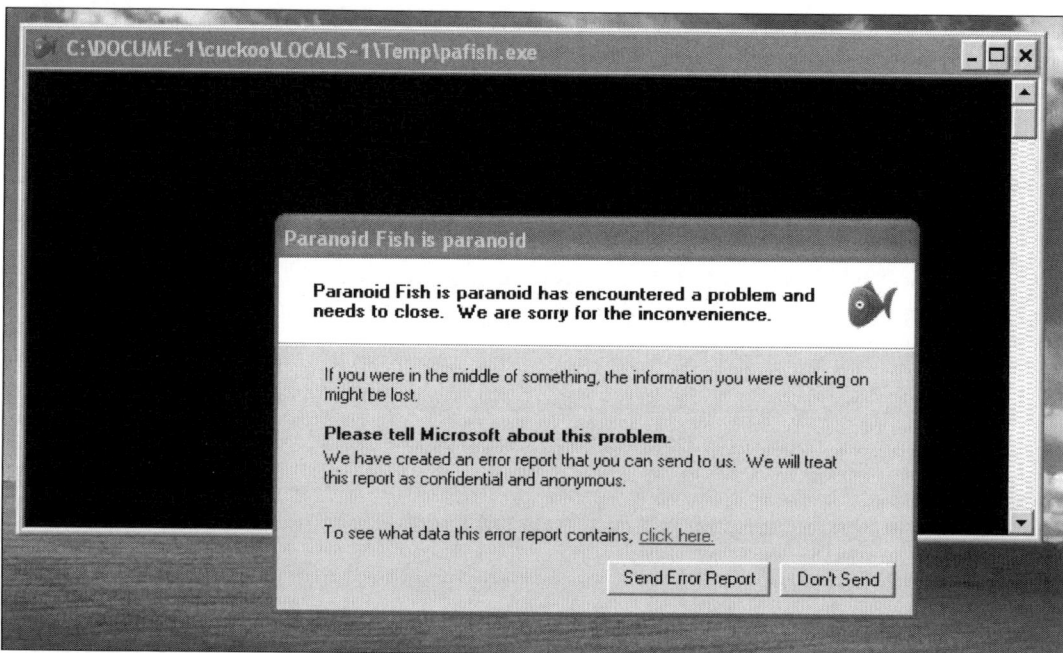

After some digging on the Internet, I found that someone named nrvana has recompiled cuckoomon.dll again. Although it is for Cuckoo Version 0.5, it turns out that it still works for Cuckoo Version 0.6, which we are using. We can download it from https://github.com/nrvana/cuckoomon.dll-0.5/blob/master/cuckoomon.dll:

```
$ sudo git clone https://github.com/nrvana/cuckoomon.dll-
0.5/blob/master/cuckoomon.dll
```

Place it into the cuckoomon folder and submit `pafish.exe` again to Cuckoo Sandbox, which is still running:

```
$ ./utils/submit.py pafish.exe
```

```
C:\DOCUME~1\cuckoo\LOCALS~1\Temp\pafish.exe                          _ □ ×
[--] Sandboxie detection
[*] Using sbiedll.dll ... OK

[--] Wine detection
[*] Using GetProcAddress(wine_get_unix_file_name) from kernel32.dll ... OK

[--] VirtualBox detection
[*] Scsi port->bus->target id->logical unit id-> 0 identifier ... OK
[*] Reg key (HKLM\HARDWARE\Description\System "SystemBiosVersion") ... OK
[*] Reg key (HKLM\SOFTWARE\Oracle\VirtualBox Guest Additions) ... OK
[*] Reg key (HKLM\HARDWARE\Description\System "VideoBiosVersion") ... traced!
[*] Looking for C:\WINDOWS\system32\drivers\VBoxMouse.sys ... OK

[--] VMware detection
[*] Scsi port->bus->target id->logical unit id-> 0 identifier ... OK
[*] Reg key (HKLM\SOFTWARE\VMware, Inc.\VMware Tools) ... OK
[*] Looking for C:\WINDOWS\system32\drivers\vmmouse.sys ... OK
[*] Looking for C:\WINDOWS\system32\drivers\vmhgfs.sys ... OK

[--] Qemu detection
[*] Scsi port->bus->target id->logical unit id-> 0 identifier ... OK
[*] Reg key (HKLM\HARDWARE\Description\System "SystemBiosVersion") ... OK

[--] Finished, feel free to RE me.
```

See, now Pafish only detects the registry key **VideoBiosVersion**. It is difficult to make all the sensors get false values, but at least we can try to reduce the detection. It is said that we can reduce about 90 percent of it.

Cuckooforcanari – integrating Cuckoo Sandbox with the Maltego project

Have you ever thought about running Cuckoo in GUI?

Yes, me too. There is a workaround for this. It is called **Cuckooforcanari** by David Bressler (@bostonlink).

It is built within **The Canari Framework** — a framework to develop Maltego written in Python. Canari is perfect for anyone wishing to graphically represent their data in Maltego without the hassle of learning a whole bunch of unnecessary stuff.

1. First, let's download and install **setuptools** before we start downloading The Canari Framework. The software can be found here:

   ```
   https://pypi.python.org/pypi/setuptools
   ```

2. Download `setuptools-0.7.7.tar.gz` and extract it:

   ```
   $ wget
   https://bitbucket.org/pypa/setuptools/raw/0.7.7/ez_setup.py -O
   - | python
   ```

3. Alternatively, in Python 2.6 and later, setuptools can be installed to a user-local path:

   ```
   $ wget
   https://bitbucket.org/pypa/setuptools/raw/0.7.7/ez_setup.py

   $ python ez_setup.py --user
   ```

4. After we've finished installing setuptools, we can install The Canari Framework by typing the following command line in the terminal:

   ```
   $ sudo easy_install canari
   ```

   That's it, now we can use Canari install package.

Before we go any further, let's make sure we have installed **Maltego**. It is an open source framework from **OSINT (Open Source Intelligence)** to gather information we look at and show how they are connected to each other. It has a nice GUI to link the relationship between various types of information and show us how they are interlinked.

We want to take this as an advantage to malware analysis to get a better picture of the information about the malware we were analyzing.

For an easy installation we could just download the `.deb` package from the Paterva website here:

```
https://www.paterva.com/web6/products/download4.php
```

First click on **MALTEGO** and then navigate to **Community (free) | Linux | DEB**.

Installing Maltego

After the `.deb` file is downloaded, you need to carry out the following steps to install Maltego:

1. Install Maltego with this command:

   ```
   $ sudo dpkg -i  maltego-radium-CE.community-2012-12-20.deb
   ```

2. Run Maltego by typing `maltego_radium_ce` in the terminal window. If Maltego doesn't run, then we need to install Java, we can install it with these commands:

   ```
   $ sudo add-apt-repository ppa:webupd8team/java
   $ sudo apt-get update
   $ sudo apt-get install oracle-java7-installer
   ```

3. Try to run Maltego.

   When you run Maltego, you will see a window which looks like the next screenshot:

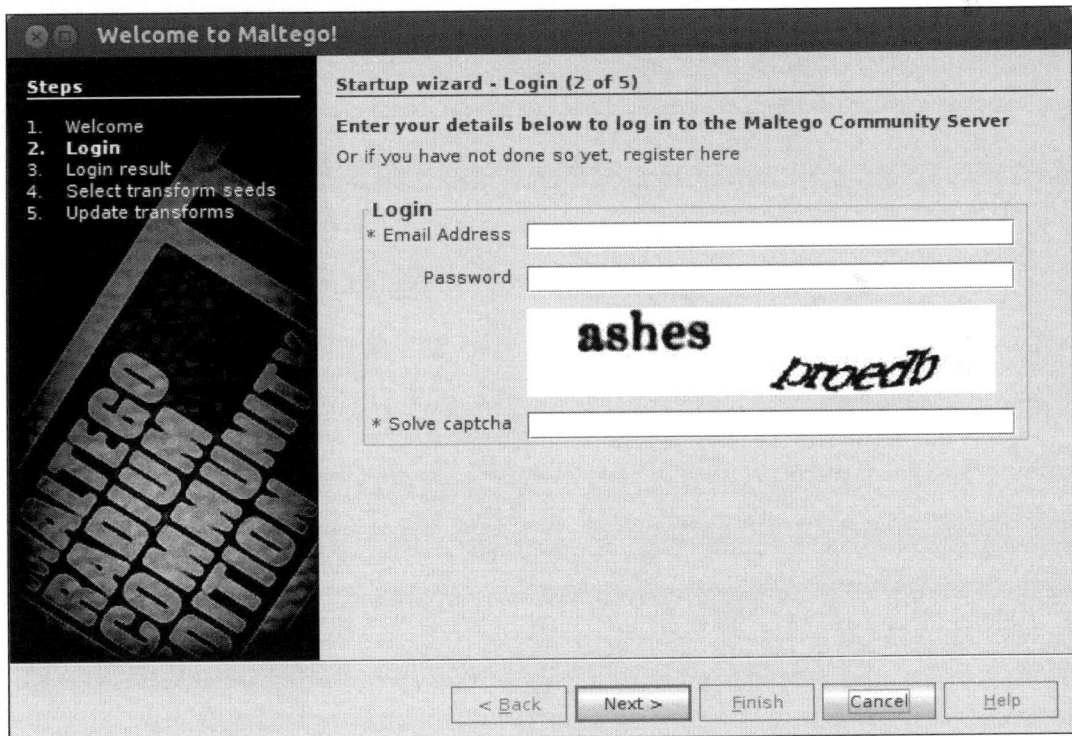

4. The preceding screenshot appears if we have never used Maltego before. If you don't have an account yet, you can choose the **register here** option and fill everything in. If everything works fine, we can continue to the main menu of Maltego.

Tada!

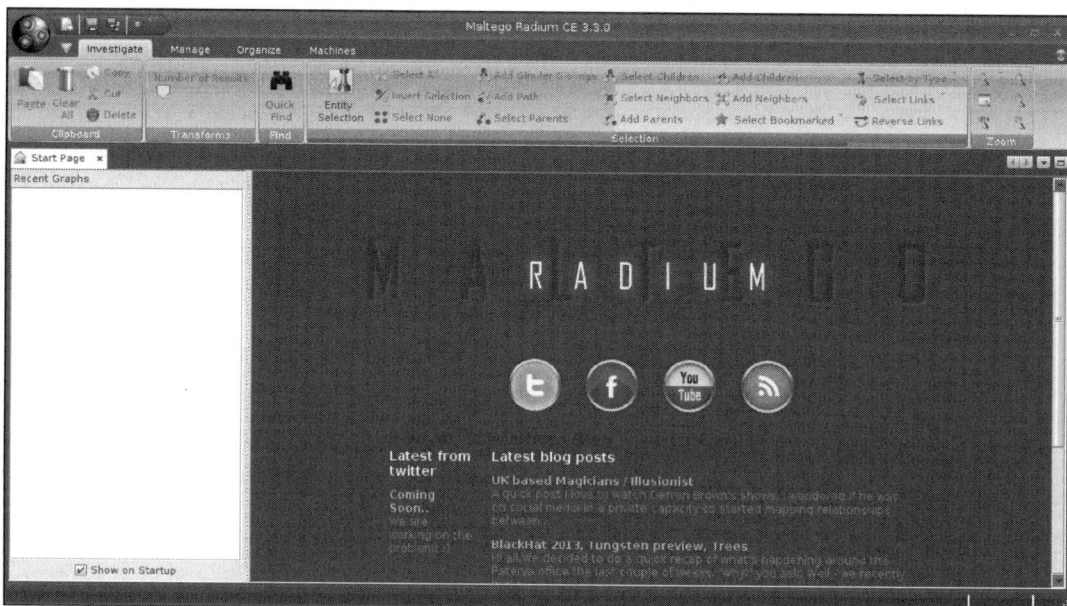

Maltego is good to go. Now, we need to download Cuckooforcanari from GitHub:

```
$ sudo mkdir cuckooforcanari
$ sudo git clone https://github.com/bostonlink/cuckooforcanari.git
cuckooforcanari/
$ python setup.py install
```

Then, we need to install the Canari package with this command line:

```
$ canari install-package cuckooforcanari
```

The Canari package will need `python-tk` as its dependency. We should install it:

```
$ sudo apt-get install python-tk
```

The last one is to change the configuration file `cuckooforcanari.conf` in folder `~/.canari/cuckooforcanari.conf`

Here is what there is inside the file:

```
# Configuration files for Cuckoo Maltego Transforms
[cuckoo]

# Cuckoo Hostname or IP address
host=localhost
# Cuckoo API port only change if you changed the API port while
starting the API. 8090 is the default
port=8090

# Malware directory - specify a directory that holds all malware
samples to be analyzed
malware_dir=/home/cuckoo/malware
```

We can use the host with any other IP address, but we can leave it as localhost because Cuckooforcanari using the Cuckoo Sandbox REST API server is running by default at localhost port 8090.

Let's run it:

```
$ ./utils/api.py
```

```
cuckoo@Ubuntu:~/cuckoo$ ./utils/api.py
Bottle server starting up (using WSGIRefServer())...
Listening on http://localhost:8090/
Hit Ctrl-C to quit.
```

Finally, the installation of Cuckooforcanari is complete. Now, we can use Cuckooforcanari in Maltego:

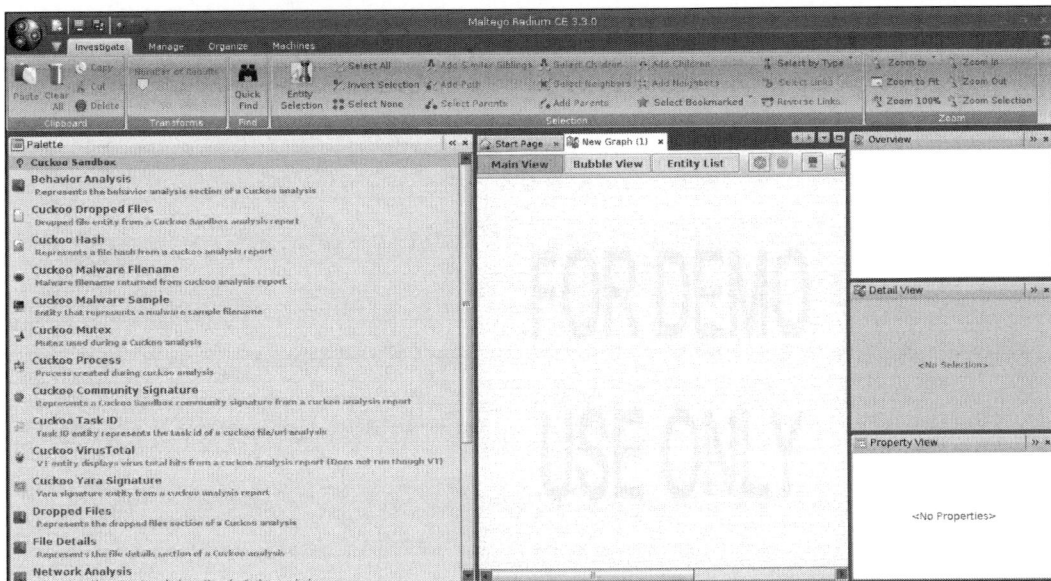

5. Look at the menu in the **Palette** tab on the left-hand side of Maltego, isn't it beautiful?

6. It becomes quite easy to work on Maltego UI. For example, drag-and-drop the **Cuckoo Malware Sample** palette into the **Main View** window.

7. Then right-click on it and choose from the pop-up menu **Run Transform | Cuckoo Sandbox | Submit file for analysis**:

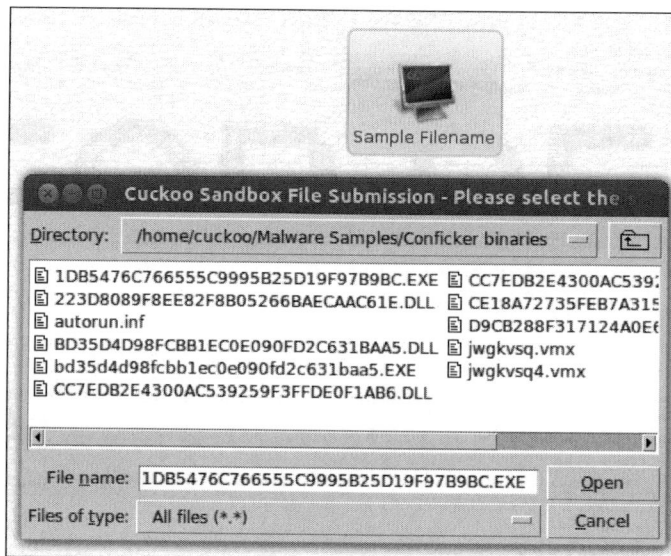

8. After submitting the analysis, we can see a picture with two cog wheels and a number. In the following screenshot, the number is **10** and this is the queue number for an analyzed file in Cuckoo Sandbox:

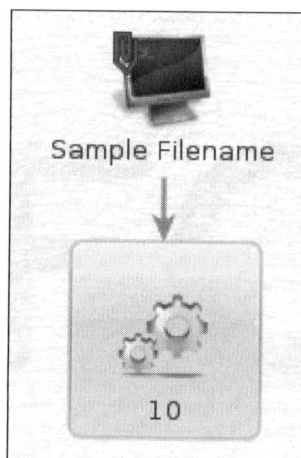

9. Now, right-click on the gearbox picture and choose **Run Transform |
    Cuckoo Sandbox | to VirusTotal results**, and see what happens. Can't
    wait, huh? Me neither.

    Maltego transform will show you something like the following screenshot:

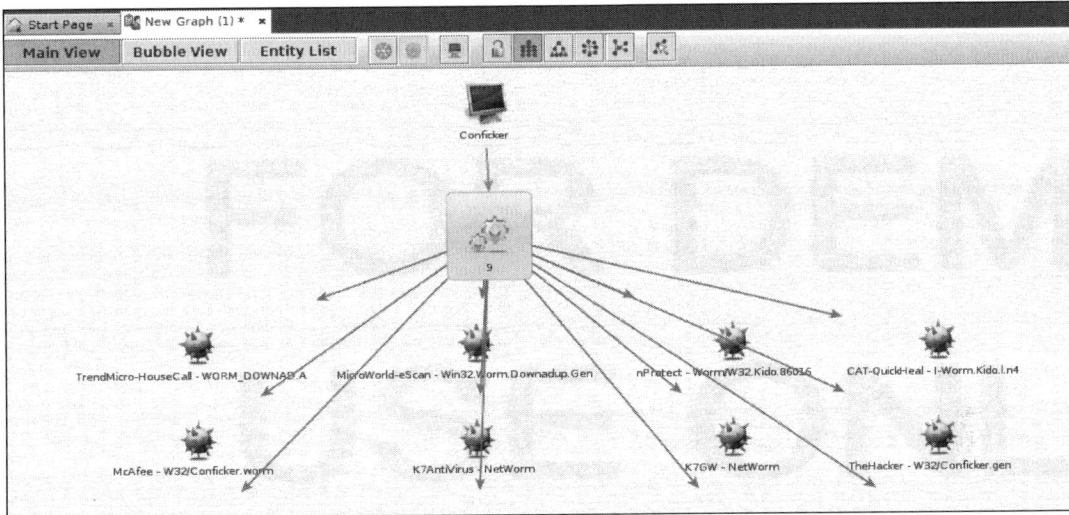

10. Let's continue to try more options. This time click on the the **Run Transform**
    option and choose **All Transforms**.

    You'll see a screenshot similar to the following:

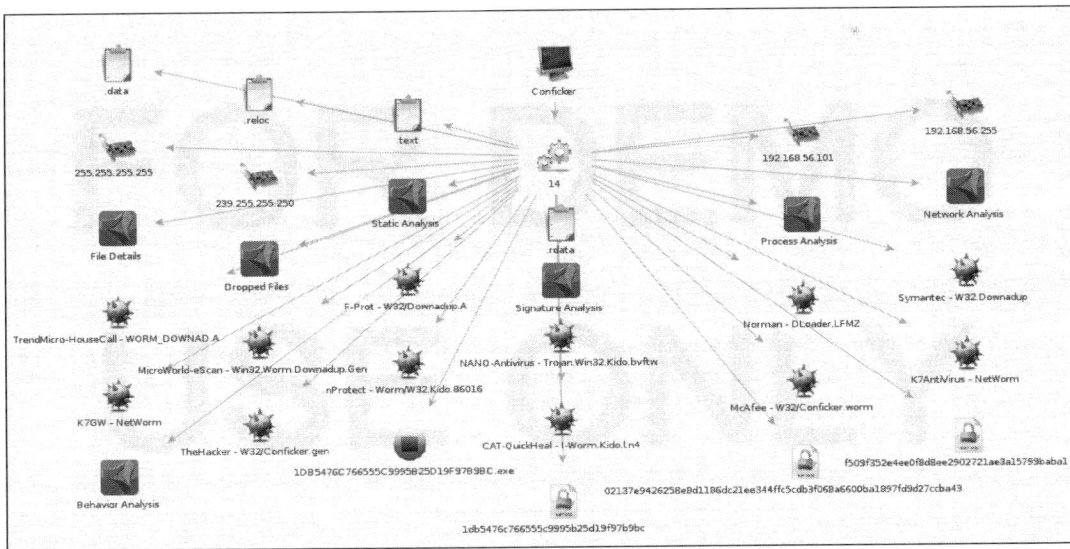

11. The following screenshot is the Maltego transform in its Hierarchical Mode:

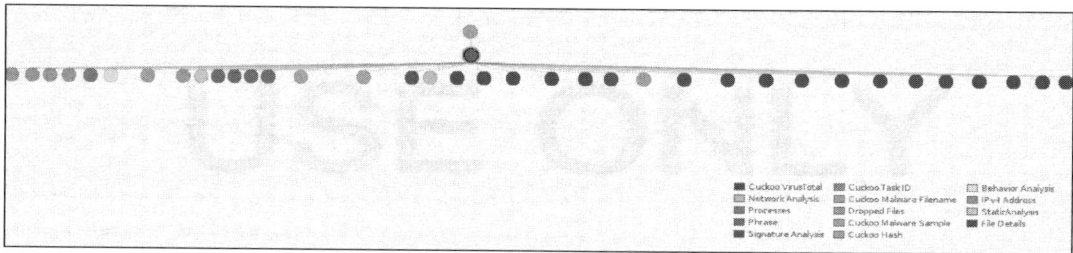

Automating e-mail attachments with Cuckoo MX

Have you ever heard about **CuckooMX**? It is a project by Xavier Mertens, you can read it at `http://blog.rootshell.be/2012/06/20/cuckoomx-automating-email-attachments-scanning-with-cuckoo/`.

CuckooMX automatically sends all the e-mail attachments to Cuckoo Sandbox, obviously, so that it can be analyzed whether the attachments—of types such as PDF, MS Office, ZIP, or other executable files—contain malware or not.

Here is a figure that might help us get a better picture of what CuckooMX does:

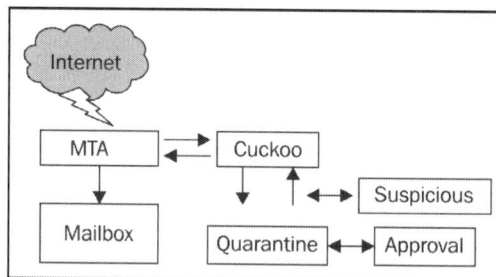

In the preceding figure, we can see that CuckooMX performs these tasks:

1. It captures the e-mail flow at **MTA (Message/Mail Transfer Agent)** level.

2. Extracts **MIME (Multipurpose Internet Mail Extensions)** attachments.

3. If it finds any PDF, MS Office, ZIP, or other executable files attached to the e-mail, that file is submitted to Cuckoo Sandbox.

4. If Cuckoo found nothing interesting and it is likely safe, it will send the attachments back to the MTA.

5. If suspicious files are found, the files will need further analysis and will need to be kept as quarantined.

CuckooMX is written in Perl and it can be downloaded from the following link:

```
https://github.com/xme/cuckoomx
```

The downloadable file contains:

- A README.txt file
- cuckoomx.conf
- cuckoomx.pl

According to the **Installation** tutorial in the **README** file, it will work with a Postfix MTA. I have not tried it with any other MTA yet. Let's try to install it to our lab. We will need:

- A running server with Postfix on it
- A running install of Cuckoo

To begin the CuckooMX installation, carry out the following steps:

1. Copy the cuckoomx.pl file into any folder of your preference, open it, and see the code starting at line 58:

```
# -----------------------------------------------------------
# Default Configuration (to be configured via cuckoomx.conf)
# -----------------------------------------------------------
My $syslogprogram      = "cuckoomx";
My $configfile            = "/home/labs/cuckoomx/cuckoomx.conf";
My $sendmailpath       = "/usr/sbin/sendmail";
My $syslogfacility       = "mail";
My $cuckoodb            = "/home/labs/cuckoo/db/cuckoo.db";
My $cuckoodir           = "/home/labs/cuckoo";
My $cuckoovm      = "labs";
My $outputdir           = "/home/labs/cuckoomx/quarantine"; #
                         Temporary directory based on our PID
My $notifyemail      = "ikons\@sandbox.com";
My $processzip           = 1;
My $processrar      = 1;
My $processurl           = 0;
```

We can see the configuration above is self-explanatory.

2. Next, copy the sample configuration file into the folder in your exact environment.

3. Edit the Postfix `master.cf` file so that the text content looks like the following:

```
# ================================================================
==========
# service type  private unprivchroot  wakeup  maxproc command +
args
#                   (yes)   (yes)   (yes)   (never) (100)
# ================================================================
==========
smtpinet  n       -       -       -       -       smtpd
-o content_filter=cuckoomx
```

And then create a new service in the bottom of the file

```
cuckoomxunix  -       n       n       -       -       pipe
user=cuckoo argv=/data/cuckoo/cuckoomx.pl -f ${sender}
${recipient}
```

4. Now let's look at the `cuckoomx.conf` file:

```
<!--
     CuckooMX Configuration File
//-->
<cuckoomx>
    <!-- Core settings //-->
    <core>
      <outputdir>/home/labs/cuckoomx/quarantine</outputdir>
        <process-zip>yes</process-zip>
        <process-rar>yes</process-rar>
        <process-url>yes</process-url>
    </core>

    <!-- Settings for Cuckoo sandbox //-->
    <cuckoo>
        <basedir>/home/labs/cuckoo</basedir>
        <db>/home/labs/cuckoo/db/cuckoo.db</db>
        <guest>WinXP-SP3</guest>
    </cuckoo>

    <!-- Logging settings //-->
    <logging>
        <syslogfacility>mail</syslogfacility>
```

```
        <sendmailpath>/usr/sbin/sendmail</sendmailpath>
        <notify>ikons@sandbox.com</notify>
    </logging>

    <!-- MIME-types to ignore (not send to Cuckoo for
      analize) //-->
    <ignore-mime>
        <mime-type>text/plain</mime-type>
        <mime-type>text/html</mime-type>
        <mime-type>image/jpeg</mime-type>
        <mime-type>image/x-citrix-jpeg</mime-type>
        <mime-type>image/png</mime-type>
        <mime-type>image/gif</mime-type>
        <mime-type>text/x-patch</mime-type>
        <mime-type>application/pkcs7-signature</mime-type>
        <mime-type>application/pgp-signature</mime-type>
        <mime-type>video/x-ms-wmv</mime-type>
        <mime-type>message/delivery-status</mime-type>
        <mime-type>text/rfc822-headers</mime-type>
    </ignore-mime>

    <!-- URLs to not process //-->
    <ignore-url>
        <url>insecure\.org</url>
        <url>secunia\.com</url>
        <url>twitter\.com</url>
        <url>(google|gmail|youtube)\.com</url>
        <url>yahoo\.com</url>
        <url>facebook\.com</url>
    </ignore-url>
</cuckoomx>
```

From the configuration settings shown in the preceding code, we only need to bring our attention to:

- `<basedir>`: This is the base directory of our Cuckoo
- `<db>`: This is the full path to the SQLite database of our Cuckoo
- `<guest>`: This is the VirtualBox Guest name to analyze malware (files)
- `<sendmailpath>`: This is the full path to the Postfix MTA binary (it is used to resend safe e-mails in the SMTP flow)

Let's try to send some e-mails to the Postfix. Now, all the e-mails received by the script is parsed and MIME attachments are extracted to a quarantine folder. If a URL, ZIP, or RAR archive is detected, files are extracted and submitted to Cuckoo. The extracted files will be generating the MD5 digest so that they can be compared to Cuckoo's DB to avoid duplication.

All of the process will be stored in `syslog`. We can see them by running the following command line in the terminal:

```
$ tail var/log/syslog
```

```
Jun 2803:13:35cuckoomxcuckoomx[15]: Processing mail from: "ikons."
<ikonspirasi@sendmail.com> (cuckoomx test)
Jun 28 03:13:35cuckoomxcuckoomx[15]: Dumped: "/home/labs/cuckoo/in/15/
msg-15-1.txt" (text/plain)
Jun 28 03:13:35cuckoomxcuckoomx[15]: Dumped: "/home/labs/cuckoo/in/15/
msg-15-2.txt" (text/plain)
Jun 28 03:13:35cuckoomxcuckoomx[15]: Dumped: "/home/labs/cuckoo/in/15/
msg-15-3.html" (text/html)
Jun 28 03:13:35cuckoomxcuckoomx[15]: Dumped: "/home/labs/cuckoo/in/15/
ikonsreport.zip" (application/zip)
Jun 28 03:13:35cuckoomxcuckoomx[15]: Files to process: 1
Jun 28 03:13:35cuckoomxcuckoomx[15]: "/home/labs/cuckoo/in/15/ikons
report.exe" already scanned (MD5: 688918c25bb714f60faf0de7c2ebc8eb)
Jun 28 03:13:35cuckoomx postfix/pipe[15]: DAC42334BFR: to=<ikons@
sandbox.com>, relay=cuckoomx, delay=0.67, delays=0.48/0/0/0.34,
dsn=2.0.0, status=sent (delivered via cuckoomx service)
```

There are some more plugins and modifications for Cuckoo Sandbox, such as Using **McAfee NTR (Network Threat Response)** with Cuckoo Sandbox (Optional) and **Collective Intelligence Framework** with Cuckoo Sandbox (Optional). So much to do, yet so little time we have. That's why we discussed only three of all the tips and tricks that Cuckoo Sandbox offers. And in the VM hardening, especially for VirtualBox, it's open source nature makes it easy to modify.

Summary

We have been playing with Cuckoo Sandbox from the start until we started VM hardening and using modifications. From this chapter, we have learned so much about VM modifications, Cuckoo Sandbox plugins for Maltego, and even automating Postfix to the Sandbox. Cuckoo Sandbox is an easy-to-use and very customizable tool, which makes it popular to the malware analysis community. Thanks to Claudio *"nex"* Guarnieri, Mark Schloesser, Alessandro *"jekil"* Tanasi, and Jurriaan Bremer — Cuckoo Sandbox developers, without them malware analysis would take so much time and make it hard to catch up to the fast growing malware development.

Index

Symbols

\<basedir\> 123
.bashrc file 67
\<db\> 123
\<guest\> 123
\<machinemanager\>.conf file 26
\<sendmailpath\> 123

A

analysis.conf file 41
analysis directory
structure 40
AnalysisInfo module 66
analysis.log file 41
APT1 attack 65
APT attack
analyzing, Cuckoo Sandbox used 74-84
analyzing, Volatility used 67, 68
analyzing, Yara used 85, 86
apt-get command 12, 96
Attached to drop-down menu 50
author server 7
automated malware analysis
implementing, drawback 8

B

BAT file 54
BehaviorAnalysis module 66
Behaviour tab 91
binary file
about 41
submitting 54-58
Bokken
about 66, 71

running, from unity dashboard 71-73
URL 66
bottlepy library 12
built-in report
creating, in HTML format 90, 91

C

Canari Framework 114
command line options
-a, --artwork 34
-d, --debug 34
-h, --help 34
-q, --quiet 34
-v, --version 34
configuration files, Cuckoo Sandbox
installation
\<machinemanager\>.conf 26
cuckoo.conf 26
processing.conf 27
reporting.conf 27-30
Continue button 40, 48
Cuckoo
about 6
data report analysis, exporting from 98-104
cuckoo.conf file 26
cuckooforcanari 113
CuckooMon source code
URL 107
CuckooMX
about 120
URL 121
Cuckoo Sandbox
about 8, 65
components 9
default configurations, modifying 68

files 9
hardening, against VM detection 105-113
installing 10
integrating, with Maltego project 113, 114
Maltego, installing 115-120
malware samples, submitting to 35-38
memory forensic, memory dump features
  used 58-61
procesing modules 66, 67
results 9
setting, in Host OS 14-16
starting 33, 34
submission utility, examples 36
used, for analyzing APT attack 74-83
Cuckoo Sandbox installation
configuration files, configuring 25
Guest OS, preparing 16, 17
hardware requirements 10
host OS, preparing 11
Python, installing in Ubuntu 11-13
requirements 11
user, creating 25
Cuckoo Scanning
e-mail attachments, automating
  with 120-124
Cuckoo Version 0.5
URL 112

D

data report analysis
exporting, from Cuckoo to another Format
  98-104
Debug module 66
Devices option 21
Download Cuckoo! button 14
dpkt library 11
Dropped Files section 54
Dropped Files tab 49, 91
Dropped module 66
dump.pcap file 41, 43
dynamic analysis 5

E

e-mail attachments
automating, with Cuckoo Scanning 120-124

F

files directory 41
File tab 43, 91

G

gedit 95
Guest OS, preparing
guest addition, installing 23
network, configuring 17-20
required specifications 16, 17
shared folder, setting up between Host OS
  and Guest OS 21, 22

H

Hosts Involved option 43
HTML format
built-in report, creating 90, 91

I

IDA Pro 71
Info tab 91
installation, Volatility 67

J

jinja2 library 11

L

libvirt library 12
logs directory 41

M

MAEC
about 92
URL 92
MAEC Report
creating 92-97
magic library 11
malicious URL
http*//ziti.cndesign.com/biaozi/fdc/
  page_07.htm 52-54
submitting 49-54

reports directory 41
REST API utility 38
run() function 101

S

Sality 57
Sality.G.exe, binary file
  submitting 54-58
Sality.G.exe screenshot 58
sandboxing 6
screenshots tab 91
self.analysis_path attribute 101
self.conf_path attribute 101
self.options attribute 101
self.reports_path attribute 101
Settings option 20
shellcode 76
shots directory 41
signatures tab 91
snapshot 8
ssdeep library 11
static analysis 5
StaticAnalysis module 66
Static Analysis section 57
static analysis tab 91
Strings module 67
submit.py utility 38
Success message 39, 44, 47, 51-55, 59

T

Take Snapshot button 33
TargetInfo module 67
Terminal tab 44, 47
TreeLine
  installing 95, 96

V

virtualbox.conf file 51
VirusShare.com 65
VirusTotal module 67, 77
VirusTotal section 46, 49, 56, 60
Volatility
  about 58, 66
  installing 67
  URL 66
  used, for analyzing APT attack 67, 68
  used, for memory forensic 62, 63
  using, steps 63
Volatility Framework tool 62

W

Wireshark
  about 66
  URL 66
Wireshark packet analyzer 43
wkhtmltopdf
  installing 98

X

Xavier Mertens
  URL 120

Y

Yara
  about 66
  URL 66
  used, for analyzing APT attack 85, 86
yara library 12
yara python library 12
Yara rule
  downloading 68-70

[PACKT] PUBLISHING   open source
community experience distilled

Thank you for buying
Cuckoo Malware Analysis

About Packt Publishing

Packt, pronounced 'packed', published its first book *"Mastering phpMyAdmin for Effective MySQL Management"* in April 2004 and subsequently continued to specialize in publishing highly focused books on specific technologies and solutions.

Our books and publications share the experiences of your fellow IT professionals in adapting and customizing today's systems, applications, and frameworks. Our solution based books give you the knowledge and power to customize the software and technologies you're using to get the job done. Packt books are more specific and less general than the IT books you have seen in the past. Our unique business model allows us to bring you more focused information, giving you more of what you need to know, and less of what you don't.

Packt is a modern, yet unique publishing company, which focuses on producing quality, cutting-edge books for communities of developers, administrators, and newbies alike. For more information, please visit our website: www.packtpub.com.

About Packt Open Source

In 2010, Packt launched two new brands, Packt Open Source and Packt Enterprise, in order to continue its focus on specialization. This book is part of the Packt Open Source brand, home to books published on software built around Open Source licenses, and offering information to anybody from advanced developers to budding web designers. The Open Source brand also runs Packt's Open Source Royalty Scheme, by which Packt gives a royalty to each Open Source project about whose software a book is sold.

Writing for Packt

We welcome all inquiries from people who are interested in authoring. Book proposals should be sent to author@packtpub.com. If your book idea is still at an early stage and you would like to discuss it first before writing a formal book proposal, contact us; one of our commissioning editors will get in touch with you.

We're not just looking for published authors; if you have strong technical skills but no writing experience, our experienced editors can help you develop a writing career, or simply get some additional reward for your expertise.

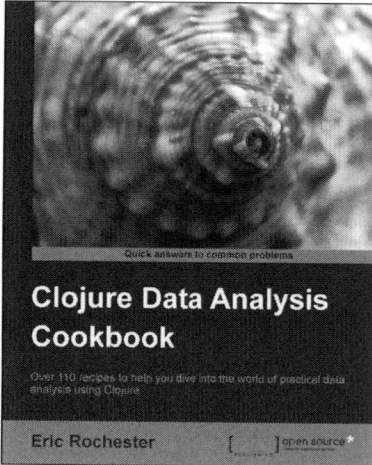

Clojure Data Analysis Cookbook

ISBN: 978-1-78216-264-3   Paperback: 342 pages

Over 110 recipes to help you dive into the world of practical data analysis using Clojure

1. Get a handle on the torrent of data the modern Internet has created

2. Recipes for every stage from collection to analysis

3. A practical approach to analyzing data to help you make informed decisions

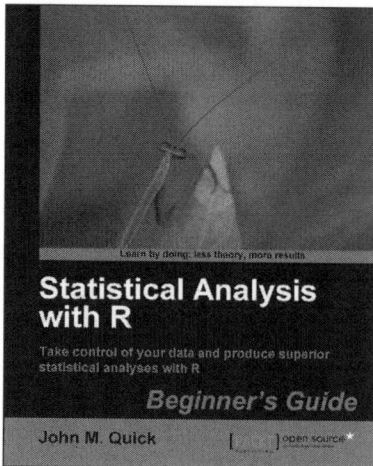

Statistical Analysis with R

ISBN: 978-1-84951-208-4   Paperback: 300 pages

Take control of your data and produce superior statistical analyses with R

1. An easy introduction for people who are new to R, with plenty of strong examples for you to work through

2. This book will take you on a journey to learn R as the strategist for an ancient Chinese kingdom!

3. A step by step guide to understand R, its benefits, and how to use it to maximize the impact of your data analysis

Please check **www.PacktPub.com** for information on our titles

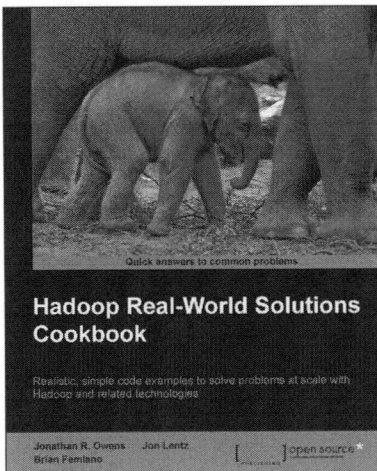

Hadoop Real-World Solutions Cookbook

ISBN: 978-1-84951-912-0   Paperback: 316 pages

Realistic, simple code examples to solve problems at scale with Hadoop and related technologies

1. Solutions to common problems when working in the Hadoop environment

2. Recipes for (un)loading data, analytics, and troubleshooting

3. In depth code examples demonstrating various analytic models, analytic solutions, and common best practices

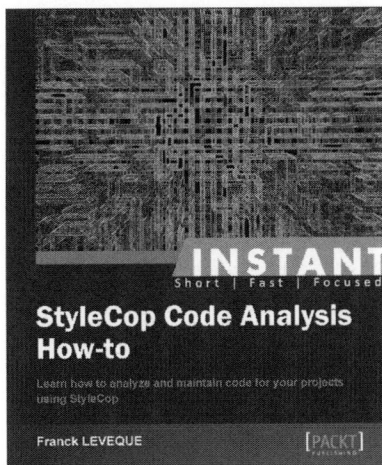

Instant StyleCop Code Analysis How-to

ISBN: 978-1-78216-954-3   Paperback: 56 pages

Learn how to analyze and maintain code for your projects using StyleCop

1. Learn something new in an Instant! A short, fast, focused guide delivering immediate results

2. Create your own custom rule for the StyleCop engine

3. Check and maintain a C# coding style over your projects

4. Personalize Microsoft rules to fit your needs

Please check **www.PacktPub.com** for information on our titles

8939200R00080

Printed in Great Britain
by Amazon.co.uk, Ltd.,
Marston Gate.